# Opiates

# Opiates

# Other books in the History of Drugs series:

# Opiates

EDITED BY NANCY HARRIS

Bruce Glassman, *Vice President*

Bonnie Szumski, *Publisher*

Helen Cothran, *Managing Editor*

**GREENHAVEN PRESS**

*An imprint of Thomson Gale, a part of The Thomson Corporation*

Detroit • New York • San Francisco • San Diego • New Haven, Conn.
Waterville, Maine • London • Munich

*For more information, contact*
Greenhaven Press
27500 Drake Rd.
Farmington Hills, MI 48331-3535
Or you can visit our Internet site at http://www.gale.com

Cover credit: © TEK Image/Science Photo Library. A hypodermic needle and syringe lay next to a pile of heroin powder.

**LIBRARY OF CONGRESS CATALOGING-IN-PUBLICATION DATA**

Opiates / Nancy Harris, book editor.
  p. cm. — (The history of drugs)
  Includes bibliographical references and index.
  ISBN 0-7377-2849-3 (lib. : alk. paper)
    1. Narcotics—History. 2. Narcotic habit—History. I. Harris, Nancy, 1952– .
  II. Series.
  RM328.O64 2005
  362.29'3—dc22                                  2004060650

Printed in the United States of America

# CONTENTS

capitalizing on opium, including cultivating it illegally and sneaking it out of town by railway or boat.

## Chapter 2: Opiates in the Twentieth Century

Department of Corrections reports on the heroin epidemic in Washington, D.C., and other cities.

## CHAPTER 3: OPIATES TODAY

so that doctors can control the withdrawal symptoms.

Drugs are chemical compounds that affect the functioning of the body and the mind. While the U.S. Food, Drug, and Cosmetic Act defines drugs as substances intended for use in the cure, mitigation, treatment, or prevention of disease, humans have long used drugs for recreational and religious purposes as well as for healing and medicinal purposes. Depending on context, then, the term *drug* provokes various reactions. In recent years, the widespread problem of substance abuse and addiction has often given the word *drug* a negative connotation. Nevertheless, drugs have made possible a revolution in the way modern doctors treat disease. The tension arising from the myriad ways drugs can be used is what makes their history so fascinating. Positioned at the intersection of science, anthropology, religion, therapy, sociology, and cultural studies, the history of drugs offers intriguing insights on medical discovery, cultural conflict, and the bright and dark sides of human innovation and experimentation.

Drugs are commonly grouped in three broad categories: over-the-counter drugs, prescription drugs, and illegal drugs. A historical examination of drugs, however, invites students and interested readers to observe the development of these categories and to see how arbitrary and changeable they can be. A particular drug's status is often the result of social and political forces that may not necessarily reflect its medicinal effects or its potential dangers. Marijuana, for example, is currently classified as an illegal Schedule I substance by the U.S. federal government, defining it as a drug with a high potential for abuse and no currently accepted medical use. Yet in 1850 it was included in the *U.S. Pharmacopoeia* as a medicine, and solutions and tinctures containing cannabis were frequently prescribed for relieving pain and inducing sleep. In the 1930s, after smokable marijuana had gained notoriety as a recreational intoxicant, the Federal Bureau of Narcotics launched a misinformation campaign against the drug, claiming that it commonly induced insanity and murderous violence. While today's medical experts no longer make such claims about marijuana, they continue to disagree about the drug's long-term effects and medicinal potential. Most interestingly, several states have passed medical marijuana initiatives, which allow seriously ill patients compassionate access to the drug under state law—although these patients can still be prosecuted for marijuana use under federal law. Marijuana's illegal status, then, is not as fixed or final as the federal government's current schedule might suggest. Examining marijuana from a historical perspective offers readers the chance to develop a more sophisticated and critically informed view of a controversial and politically charged subject. It also encourages students to learn about aspects of medicine, history, and culture that may receive scant attention in textbooks.

Each book in Greenhaven's The History of Drugs series chronicles a particular substance or group of related drugs—discussing the appearance and earliest use of the drug in initial chapters and more recent and contemporary controversies in later chapters. With the incorporation of both primary and secondary sources written by physicians, anthropologists, psychologists, historians, social analysts, and lawmakers, each anthology provides an engaging panoramic view of its subject. Selections include a variety of readings, including book excerpts, government documents, newspaper editorials, academic articles, and personal narratives. The editors of each volume aim to include accounts of notable incidents, ideas, subcultures, or individuals connected with the drug's history as well as perspectives on the effects, benefits, dangers, and legal status of the drug.

Every volume in the series includes an introductory essay that presents a broad overview of the drug in question. The annotated table of contents and comprehensive index help readers quickly locate material of interest. Each selection is prefaced by a summary of the article that also provides any necessary historical context and biographical information on the author. Several other research aids are also present, including excerpts of supplementary material, a time line of relevant historical events, the U.S. government's current drug schedule, a fact sheet detailing drug effects, and a bibliography of helpful sources.

Greenhaven Press's The History of Drugs series gives readers a unique and informative introduction to an often-ignored facet of scientific and cultural history. The contents of each anthology provide a valuable resource for general readers as well as for students interested in medicine, political science, philosophy, and social studies.

Opiates are drugs derived from the opium poppy, *Papaver som-niferum*. The most well-known opiates are opium, morphine, codeine, and heroin. These drugs are classified as narcotics: drugs that relieve pain, dull the senses, induce sleep, and are often addictive. Opium is a raw natural product, the dried juice of the unripe capsule of the opium poppy. It contains at least thirty-five alkaloids, organic substances that have alkaline properties and contain nitrogen. These include morphine and codeine. Morphine is the chief active ingredient in opium; codeine is found in opium in small amounts.

Heroin (diacetylmorphine) is produced by heating mor-phine in the presence of acetic acid (a substance found in vinegar). It is sometimes called a semisynthetic opiate, be-cause it is derived from opium but has undergone chemical modification. Heroin acts more quickly than morphine be-cause it is absorbed by the brain from the blood much more easily. Heroin is converted back into morphine after it is intro-duced into the body but not before a small amount reaches the brain and produces physiological and psychological effects.

Another group of drugs related to the opiates are the opi-oids, drugs that activate the opioid receptors found in the brain, spinal cord, or intestines. The opioids include natural opiates that are drugs derived from the opium poppy and semisynthetic and synthetic opiates. Synthetic opiates are drugs that are manufactured to have similar properties and effects as natural opiates. Methadone (Dolophine) and propoxyphene (Darvon) are synthetic opiates. Examples of semisynthetic opiates be-sides heroin are meperidine (Demerol) and oxycodone (Perco-dan, Percocet, and OxyContin). Chemists created synthetic and semisynthetic opiates to provide analgesics (painkillers) that would not produce drug dependence. However, it was found that all opiates (or opioids) can be addictive.

Opiates have been used for thousands of years in a variety

of beneficial ways: medicinally, socially, in religious practices, and in cooking. However, while opiates have many positive uses, people who become addicted to them suffer their severe consequences.

## Positive Uses for Opiates

Ancient people found many positive uses for opium. Anthropologists believe opium was used by the Sumerians as long ago as the fourth millennium B.C. Opium may be the only drug used by doctors in ancient times that is still used today. Egyptian doctors treated patients with opium before 200 B.C. and Egyptian priests used opium in their religious ceremonies. In Greek and Roman times opium was commonplace and was used medicinally as well as in religious and occult practices. By the eleventh century opium was being eaten as a household remedy by all classes in India, and in China opium seeds were widely used for their medicinal benefits. Paracelsus (1493–1541), believed by some to be the father of modern medicine, was the first in the Western world to acknowledge the therapeutic properties of opium. He introduced laudanum, a mixture of opium and alcohol, into pharmacology and prescribed it as a painkiller.

By the late 1600s opium's popularity led well-known English chemist Thomas Sydenham to comment: "Among the remedies which it has pleased the Almighty God to give man to relieve his sufferings, none is so universal and efficacious as opium."[1] Indeed, physicians prescribed opium not only for pain but for coughs, diarrhea, dysentery, and a host of other illnesses. Opium was used in a variety of preparations including Dover's powder, created by the British doctor Thomas Dover, and used for the next 150 years as a treatment for gout. Physicians in the early 1800s believed that chemists had perfected opium with the introduction of morphine, referring to it as "God's own medicine" or "G.O.M." Morphine supplanted the use of raw opium for medicinal purposes mainly because of its tranquilizing properties, but also in part because of its reliability, safety, and long-lasting effects. In an 1880 textbook, morphine injection was listed as being effective against fifty-four diseases including anemia, diabetes, insanity, tetanus, and nymphomania. In addition, nineteenth-century doctors recommended morphine as a treatment for alcohol abuse. Doctors reasoned that using morphine to treat alcohol addiction would replace one evil habit with a lesser one. Morphine's calming effects on alcoholics reduced their violent behavior, and when alcoholics used morphine they no longer experienced the medical problems related to alcoholism, including cirrhosis of the liver, jaundice, and acute gastritis. Consequently, many physicians in the United States used morphine to treat alcoholism until the 1940s.

When physicians first prescribed heroin in 1898 in Germany, it was used therapeutically as an unrivaled cough suppressant. For many years heroin was the main ingredient in several over-the-counter cough syrups. Indeed, it was widely endorsed as a miracle medicine and was used for treating chest pains, pneumonia, and tuberculosis. Physicians today continue to use heroin medicinally, though not in the United States or Canada. As medical journalist Mark Pownall notes, "Pure heroin (diamorphine) is used in some countries as a way of killing pain after accidents, after surgical operations, or when someone is suffering from pain caused by an illness such as cancer. It is one of the strongest painkillers available. Pure heroin is not, in itself, very harmful."[2] As morphine was heralded as a treatment for opium abuse in the nineteenth century, heroin was lauded as a cure for morphine addiction in the beginning of the twentieth century. In the United States the philanthropic Saint James Society carried on a campaign in the early 1900s to supply free samples of heroin through the mail to morphine addicts.

As a result of their beneficial effects and popularity, opiates in the nineteenth century were legal, cheap, and as accessible as aspirin is today. Although there were some in American and

British society who considered taking them a personal vice and even immoral, there were no laws banning opiates because the public did not view their use as threatening. Well-known British writers such as John Keats experimented with opium recreationally, taking it for its mood-altering effects but only in doses that were nonaddictive. However, other British writers such as Thomas De Quincey and Samuel Coleridge admitted to having developed opium and laudanum habits but believed that taking opiates increased their creativity and helped them to produce their finest works.

## Negative Uses of Opiates

Opiate users reaped many benefits from using these drugs; however, some suffered negative effects as well. In the Middle Ages, doctors in Arabia, Persia, Turkey, China, and India warned of opium's addictiveness. By the late nineteenth century in the United States, some physicians liberally prescribed large amounts of opiates and were addicted themselves. In addition, drug companies produced far more of the drugs than were needed for medical use. As a result, by the early twentieth century, according to historian Alfred W. McCoy, opium, morphine, and heroin had become a major global commodity equivalent in scale to products such as coffee and tea. In the United States and England at this time, people began to condemn the expansion of opiate use and inspired a global anti-opium movement that resulted in the passage of the first drug laws. In 1905 Congress prohibited opium for any purpose other than medical use, and in 1924 the Heroin Act made the manufacture of heroin illegal. These laws were created to eliminate the sources for nonmedical use of opiates and to punish opiate abusers. As educators Daniel A. Girando and Dorothy Dusek Girando observe, "Historically, it has been opium and its derivatives (morphine, heroin, and codeine) that have generated the deep fear of addiction and of addicts in our country. Our first drug laws were made basically to rid the country of such drugs and the deviant behavior stemming from them."[3]

Some question the efficacy of these laws, pointing to the fact that when opiates were made illegal, those who remained addicted to the drugs resorted to obtaining their supply from criminals. Formerly viewed as a personal vice or weakness, opiate use became a criminal activity. Addicts themselves were seen as criminals for violating drug laws and for resorting to violent crime and theft to support their habit as the price of opiates, especially heroin, became exorbitant. Increased crime rates were accompanied by expanding international drug rings and smuggling. As smuggling became increasingly difficult, traffickers favored more potent opiates such as heroin over morphine and opium because they could make the same profits from smaller amounts of drugs. Users began injecting rather than drinking opiates because it gave them a greater high. Sharing needles for intravenous heroin use resulted in the spread of HIV/AIDS and hepatitis. In addition, the unreliable quality and unpredictable purity of drugs sold on the black market led to poisoning and accidental overdoses.

Today in the United States, authorities say that more people are using heroin than any other opiate; however, according to the National Survey on Drug Use and Health, the number of heroin users did drop from 166,000 in 2002 to 119,000 in 2003, although heroin use has increased in some locations such as New York City. The number of hardcore heroin addicts is hard to establish, but authorities estimate that each year 1 percent of serious heroin addicts die of overdose. According to the National Institute on Drug Abuse, recent studies show that heroin users have shifted from injecting heroin to snorting or smoking it because of the drug's increased purity and the misconception that these forms of use will not lead to addiction. On the contrary, with prolonged use heroin users develop a tolerance and must use more of the drug to get the same pleasurable effects. The user must constantly seek out a supply of heroin because abstinence means withdrawal, and withdrawal means physical pain and mental anguish. Heroin users may suffer withdrawal effects including insomnia, muscle spasms, cold sweats, and abdominal cramps. They may feel an overwhelming craving for heroin's mood-altering effects because they have taken the drug to relieve anxiety and depression and have developed a psychological dependence on it.

Heroin and other opiate users all over the world suffer these types of drug dependencies. In addition to drug addiction problems, some countries face the issues of illegal opium poppy cultivation and opium and heroin production. Although production of opium and heroin in the Asian opium zone, including countries such as Afghanistan, Turkey, Thailand, Burma, and Laos, has fluctuated over past decades, opium poppies continue to be a major crop in these countries, partly due to extreme poverty. In the words of Afghan Muslim teacher Abdul Rashid, "Of course we believe that growing this poppy will have a very bad moral effect on the people. . . . In the future, we hope it will be eradicated. Now, it's everywhere because the people need it to survive."[4]

The beneficial uses of opiates have a long history that is intricately entwined with the history of its harmful effects. Although the inherent qualities of opiates have never changed, cultural attitudes and uses have. While opium was once viewed as a socially benign and even sacred substance, some of its alkaloids and derivatives have become serious criminal and social health problems.

## Notes

1. Quoted in Julian Durlacher, *Heroin: Its History and Lore*. London: Carlton, 2000, p. 72.

2. Mark Pownall, *Drugs, the Complete Story: Heroin*. Austin, TX: Steck-Vaugh, 1992, p. 8.

3. Daniel A. Girando and Dorothy Dusek Girando, *Drug Education: Content and Methods*. Reading, MA: Addison-Wesley, 1972, p. 154.

4. Quoted in April Witt, "Afghan Poppies Proliferate," *Washington Post*, July 10, 2003, p. A01.

# CHAPTER ONE

# Early Opiates

# An Overview of Early Opium Use

*Martin Booth*

Naturally occurring opium has been used since prehistoric times. In this selection Martin Booth describes where and how opium was first used. Booth says that the first opium poppy remains were found in sites of fourth-millennium B.C. villages in Switzerland, and that the Sumerians, the world's first agriculturists, were believed to have cultivated the opium poppy in 3400 B.C. Eventually, Booth says, doctors used opium as a cure for many ailments. The Greeks used it medicinally as well as for spiritual or occult practices. They also mixed it with alcohol and used it as a tranquilizer to banish fear, anguish, and troubling memories. The Greeks passed their knowledge of opium on to the Romans, who saw opium as a powerful symbol of sleep and death. The Romans used opium not only as a painkiller and for religious purposes but as a poison for suicide and assassinations. Neither the Greeks nor the Romans traded opium as a major commodity, but by the ninth century the Arabs had organized the production and trade of opium. Martin Booth is a novelist, poet, and nonfiction writer. He is the author of *Hiroshima Joe, Adrift in the Oceans of Mercy*, and *A Very Private Gentleman.*

Opium has been used by man since prehistoric times and was arguably the first drug to be discovered. Being naturally occurring, it almost certainly predates the discovery of alcohol which requires a knowledge of fermentation.

The preserved remains of cultivated poppy seeds and pods have been discovered in the sites of fourth millennium B.C. Neolithic pile-dwelling villages in Switzerland. Botanical examination has shown these not to be *Papaver setigerum*, but *P. somniferum* [today's opium poppy] or possibly a deliberate hybrid. As these ancient farmers also grew linseed, it is likely both crops were utilised for their oil although no suitable contemporary tools for oil extraction have been found and it is, therefore, just as likely the poppy was grown for its narcotic effect, either as a painkiller or for use in religious ceremonies—or for both.

It has long been suggested that the knowledge of opium spread from Egypt through Asia Minor to the rest of the Old World but the Swiss discoveries cast this theory into doubt. What is as likely is that the secret of opium originated in the eastern reaches of Europe—in the Balkans or around the Black Sea—and spread south and west from there.

Around 3400 B.C., the opium poppy was being cultivated in the Tigris-Euphrates river systems of lower Mesopotamia. The Sumerians, the world's first civilisation and agriculturists, used the ideograms *hul* and *gil* for the poppy, this translating as the 'joy plant'. Their invention of writing spread gradually to other societies and it is from them the Egyptians probably learnt the skill: it follows they may also have learnt of opium. It may be reasoned, therefore, that the Sumerians not only gave humankind literacy but also one of its greatest problems.

## Opium Is a Cure-All

By the end of the second millennium B.C., knowledge of opium was widespread throughout Europe, the Middle East and North Africa. Poppy juice is mentioned in seventh-century B.C. Assyrian medical tablets contained in the royal library of the Babylonian King Asurbanipal, although these are thought to be copies of earlier texts. Doctors of the time considered opium a cure for almost every ailment, sometimes mixing it with liquorice or balsam: of 115 vegetable concoctions mentioned,

42 concern opium which was collected early in the morning by women and children who scraped the congealed sap off wounds in the poppies with a small iron scoop.

Yet the earliest find of opium itself comes from Egypt where a sample was discovered in the tomb of Cha, dating to the fifteenth century B.C. At around the same time, the Egyptian city of Thebes was so famous for its poppy fields that Egyptian opium was known as Thebic opium. The alkaloid, thebaine, obtains its name from the city. In the *Therapeutic Papyrus of Thebes*, dated 1552 B.C., and in other sources such as the *Veterinary and Gynaecological Papyri* from Kahun, dated between 2160 and 1788 B.C., opium is prominently listed with other natural remedies and drugs: in the former—sometimes known as the *Papyrus of Ebers* after its discoverer, Georg Moritz Ebers—opium is included in 700 remedies, one chapter specifically prescribing it as a paregoric to calm fractious children. The prescription demanded opium be mixed with fly droppings, pulped, sieved and taken for four days.

## Opium a Commonplace in Greece

For the Greek civilisation, opium was a commonplace. In the third century B.C., [Greek philosopher] Theophrastus referred to the sap of the pod as *opion* whilst he called poppy juice *meconion*, obtained by crushing the entire plant. This is an interesting fact for it suggests he had a specific knowledge that the sap contained a substance and that he may have been acquainted with separating it out although, at the time, the general method of taking opium was to crush the pod in wine or a honey and water solution. The method of incising the pod to gather the sap, developed by the Assyrians and used to this day, was lost until the technique was re-invented or rediscovered about A.D. 40 by Scribonius Largus, physician to the Emperor Claudius.

In A.D. 77, [Greek pharmacologist] Dioscorides wrote that opium was best obtained by the careful grazing of the pod, although he was just as familiar with other applications of the poppy. He recorded:

> Poppies possess as it were a cooling power, therefore the leaves and head when boiled in water bring sleep. The decoction is also drunk to remedy insomnia. Finely powdered and added to groats, the heads make an effective poultice for swellings and erysipelas. They must be crushed when still green, shaped into tablets then dried for storage. If the heads themselves are boiled in water until the liquid is reduced to half then boiled with honey until a syrup forms, they may make a sweetmeat with an anodyne action.

Both Dioscorides and Theophrastus, whilst noting opium induced sleep and numbed pain, did not consider its effects upon the brain which were generally disregarded although the philosopher Diagoras of Melos was cognisant of the drug's snare. Living in the third century b.c., he declared it was better to suffer pain than to become dependent upon opium, a view shared earlier in the fifth century b.c. by Erasistratus who advocated the complete eschewal of opium.

## Opium's Spiritual Significance

Apart from its medicinal use, opium also served the Greeks in a spiritual or occult capacity. It was most likely employed by initiates to the cult of Demeter for there is a legend which decrees that, in her search of her daughter Persephone, the goddess came to Sicyon, at one time called Mecone (the city of poppies), in the fields of which she picked the flowers and cut open their unripe pods. Tasting the gum which exuded from them, Demeter forgot her sorrows. Statues and portraits of the goddess frequently show her grasping a poppy instead of a sheaf of corn whilst the flower decorates her altars. There is a further suggestion: in her rites conducted at Eleusis, opium was taken to aid in the forgetting of the sadness of the death of the year, the short drug-induced sleep being a symbol for the passage of winter before the rejuvenation of spring. The medical priests of Aesculapeius administered opium to those who visited Epidaurus to seek a cure for illness. The sick slept in the sanctuary of the temple, the priests procuring healing dreams for them.

## Hippocrates Says Use Opium Sparingly

As long as opium was in the hands of priests it was regarded as a metaphysical substance. This supernatural attitude, however, was dismissed by Hippocrates (460–357 B.C.). Considered the father of medicine, he disassociated himself from the magical attributes of opium which he mentioned was useful as a cathartic, hypnotic, narcotic and styptic. A reasoned and logical thinker, Hippocrates concluded diseases were naturally caused and were, therefore, cured by natural remedies. Opium was, for him, one of the latter, which he believed required study and understanding rather than being imbued with miraculous powers. He suggested drinking hypnotic meconion (white poppy juice) mixed with nettle seeds to cure leucorrhea and 'uterine suffocation'. Like [Greek poet] Diagoras, Hippocrates was of the opinion it should be used sparingly and under control, a stipulation which exists to this day in the Hippocratic oath which states, 'I will give no deadly medicine to anyone if asked, nor suggest any such counsel.'

## Opium in Literature

It was not long before opium began to appear in literature. In the *Odyssey*, Homer writes of 'nepenthe', the drug of forgetfulness, which was an opium preparation. When Telemachus visited Menelaus in Sparta, the memory of Ulysses and the other warriors lost in the Trojan War so saddened the gathering a banquet was commanded for which Helen prepared a special cordial:

> Helen, daughter of Zeus, poured a drug, nepenthe, into the wine they were drinking which made them forget all evil. Those who drank of the mixture did not shed a tear all day

long, even if their mother or father had died, even if a brother or beloved son was killed before their own eyes by the weapons of the enemy. And the daughter of Zeus possessed this wondrous substance which she had been given by Polydamma, the wife of Thos of Egypt, the fertile land which produced so many balms, some beneficial and some deadly.

## THE HISTORY OF DRUGS

# The Opium Poppy

*Opium from the poppy* Papaver somniferum *has been used medicinally and recreationally for many centuries. It contains numerous alkaloids, including papaverine, morphine, codeine, and thebaine.*

When the unripe seed capsule of the opium poppy, *Papaver somniferum*, is cut or pricked, a viscous liquid is exuded. After the exudate dries and darkens with exposure to air, a hard but still partly sticky mass is obtained. This is opium, which has been used for many centuries by some for medicinal purposes and by others to smoke in their pipes, reaching, we are told, most pleasant Elysian fields of sensation, albeit addicting and enslaving.

The pharmacologically active constituents of opium have been employed in medicine for many thousands of years in the form of a highly colored tincture. During the nineteenth century these constituents were isolated as pure chemical entities [alkaloids].

Papaverine, the simplest structurally, is used with excellent results as a muscle relaxant. Morphine is used as an analgesic which even today has no peer in controlling severe pain. Codeine is used as a more specialized analgesic and as an effective agent for the control of the cough reflex. Thebaine is too toxic to be used as such but has served as a starting material for the synthesis of more specific analgesics which have rather limited medicinal uses.

David Ginsburg, *The Opium Alkaloids*. New York: Interscience Publishers, 1962, p. 1.

Homer's noting opium came from Egypt is hardly surprising: not only had this source been known of for centuries but Egyptian doctors were renowned. Even Moses shared their secret as was recorded in the Bible, Acts 7, verse 22: 'And Moses was learned in all the wisdom of the Egyptians, and was mighty in words and in deeds.'

For a long while, scholars assumed nepenthe was hashish but this is incorrect. What is plainly described is the effect of opium which, especially once established as a habit, promotes indifference towards everything except the ego and a calm euphoria in which anger and sorrow are suppressed. Hashish, on the other hand, usually produces a delirious excitement.

Homer's description was not a matter of poetic licence. He was writing about an everyday experience undergone by those addicted and it is almost certain the poet had taken opium, even if he was not habituated. Furthermore, a solution of opium in alcohol was used by the Greeks as a tranquilliser, to banish fear, anguish and hateful memories: it might also have been used to promote Dutch courage in warriors going into battle. The tradition of opium as an antidote to sorrow lingers to the modern day: in some places in the Middle East, iced poppy tea is traditionally served to mourners at funerals.

## Opium in Rome

When the Greek civilisation was usurped by the Empire of Rome, more than works of art and treasure were plundered and brought to Italy. So, too, came learning, including the knowledge of opium, spread by military men returning from foreign campaigns (including those in Egypt and the Middle East), priests, physicians, intellectuals and Greek slaves many of whom were educated and employed in Rome as tutors and administrators.

Galen, in the first and second centuries A.D., was the last of the great Greek physicians. Although he considered it to be influenced by the occult, he did not claim direct magical properties for opium but he did afford it the omniscient properties of a glorious panacea, claiming it resisted poison and venomous bites and cured, amongst other things, headaches, vertigo, deafness, epilepsy, apoplexy, poor sight, bronchitis, asthma, coughs, the spitting of blood, colic, jaundice, hardness of the spleen, kidney stones, urinary complaints, fever, dropsy, leprosy, menstrual problems, melancholy and all other pestilences. It was he who popularised the use of one of the famous early opium concoctions, *mithridate*, the invention of which is accorded to Mithridates the Great. Galen advocated it to all his patients amongst whom were numbered Marcus Aurelius and the Emperors Commodus and Severus. Yet, for all his apparent quackery, Galen was a serious scientist. He studied and published his findings on the toxic effects of opium and understood the concept of tolerance—that is, the ability of the body to withstand larger and larger successive doses, requiring increasing doses to gain the same effect as time goes by.

Like Homer, Virgil mentioned opium in his works: in both the *Aeneid* and the *Georgics* it is mentioned as a soporific. His lines *spargens humida melle soperiferumque paparva* (giving dewy honey and soporific poppy) and *Lethaeo perfusa papavera somno* (poppies soaked with the sleep of Lethe) indicate very clearly the accepted capabilities of the drug. Pliny the Elder wrote that poppy seed (he was incorrect) was a useful hypnotic, whilst the poppy latex was effective in treating headaches and arthritis and in healing wounds.

## The Poppy as a Symbol of Sleep and Death

For the Romans, the poppy was a powerful symbol of sleep and death. Somnus, the god of sleep, is frequently portrayed as a small boy or sprite carrying a bunch of poppies and an opium horn, the vessel in which the juice was collected by farmers, whilst another popular image is that of a figure bending over a woman and pouring poppy juice on to her closed eyes. The poppy also formed part of the mysteries of Ceres, the

Roman goddess of fertility, who resorted to the drug to relieve pain: a famous statue shows her holding a torch and poppy pods. Indeed, the poppy was so well known a symbol that, in later years of the empire, it was to be found on Roman coinage.

The Romans viewed opium not only as a painkiller and religious drug but as a convenient poison. For the suicide, it was a pleasant means of enticing death. [Carthaginian general] Hannibal was said to have kept a dose in a small chamber in his ring, finally ending his life with it in Libyssa in 183 B.C. Yet its main attraction was for the murderer.

Being easily obtained, easily disguised in food or dissolved in wine and bringing a seemingly innocent death as if in sleep, opium poisoning was an ideal assassin's aid. According to the historian Cornelius Nepos, the son of Dionysius (the tyrant of Syracuse) arranged with the court doctors in 367 B.C. for his father to overdose on opium. In A.D. 55 Agrippina, the Emperor Claudius's last wife, put it into the wine of her fourteen-year-old stepson, Britannicus, so her own son, Nero, might inherit the throne.

As a medicine, opium was taken in a number of concoctions but for leisure use—as what would now be termed a 'recreational drug'—it was eaten often mixed with honey to suppress its bitterness.

The eating of opium increased as the knowledge of its beneficial properties became more widely known. In the second century A.D., it was stated that Lysis could take 4 drachms of poppy juice without being incommoded. To be so tolerant of the drug suggests he was a well-established addict: such a quantity would have killed a first-time imbiber.

Curiously, neither the Greeks nor the Romans spread the use of opium throughout the whole of their domains and they did not regard opium as an international trading commodity.

However, the Arabs did. They had used opium as a painkiller since the time of the Egyptians and it was the Arabs who developed and organised the production of, and trade in, opium which has existed ever since.

# The British and Chinese Opium Wars

*Westel Woodbury Willoughby*

The abuse of opium became a matter of international concern in the first half of the nineteenth century when conflict developed between Chinese authorities and British opium merchants. In this selection Westel Woodbury Willoughby explains that although opium was prohibited in China in the late 1700s, the British nevertheless sent large shipments of the drug from India into China because they were making large profits from the trade. Because the British continued to increase their opium shipments, Chinese authorities ultimately seized and destroyed opium held by British merchants in Canton, triggering the first Opium War in 1839. The treaty following the war compelled China to open four ports, to cede Hong Kong to the British, and to pay $6 million for the opium they had destroyed. After a second war and repeated British efforts to legalize opium imports into China, the Chinese finally gave up the struggle in 1858, accepting the legalization of the drug trade between the two countries.

Westel Woodbury Willoughby was a professor of political science at Johns Hopkins University as well as an adviser to the Chinese delegation to the Geneva Opium Conferences in 1923. His books include *Foreign Rights and Interests in China* and *China at the Conference* (in Washington, D.C.).

The poppy plant appears to have been known in China since the eighth century A.D. The medicinal value of its product,

Westel Woodbury Willoughby, *Opium as an International Problem*. Baltimore: The Johns Hopkins Press, 1925.

opium, had been known by the Chinese for several centuries, but the habit of smoking it was probably borrowed from abroad. Once introduced, the vice spread rapidly—so rapidly, indeed, that the Chinese political authorities became aroused and sought to prevent it by stringent prohibitory edicts.

The first of these edicts was issued in 1796 and four years later the importation of foreign opium was forbidden. At this time the importation of opium, almost wholly from India, had amounted to over four thousand chests annually. [A chest contains a "picul" or 133 lbs.] However, notwithstanding this prohibition, the amount of Indian opium annually introduced into China continued to increase, until, by 1838, it had reached the enormous quantity of over twenty thousand chests, and it was the drastic attempt of the Chinese authorities to deal with this grave situation that furnished the proximate as well as one of the most substantial of the causes of the war with Great Britain.

## The Opium War

Attempt has been made by some writers to show that this war was not properly termed an "Opium War," but the evidence is overwhelming that it was with justice given that name. Not only was the outbreak of hostilities due to the seizure and destruction by the Chinese authorities of certain amounts of opium held by British merchants in Canton, which, in violation of Chinese law, had been brought into China, but one of the conditions imposed upon defeated China was that she should pay an indemnity of six million dollars for the opium thus seized and destroyed. If one has any doubts upon this subject, he need only read the impartial account of the events leading up to, and the results following from, this war as given by S. Wells Williams in his scholarly treatise *The Middle Kingdom*. After hostilities had begun and the question was discussed in the British Parliament as to what action the British Government should take, the debate dealt almost wholly with the opium trade. At that time there seemed to be no question in

England as to the causes of the war. Only later was the effort made by British historians and statesmen to show that the opium question was but an incidental, and not a dominating, factor in the situation.

[British prime minister William E.] Gladstone had no doubt as to the character of the war that Great Britain had waged. Of this war he said: "A war more unjust in its origin, a war more calculated to cover this country with permanent disgrace, I do not know and have not read of. The British flag is hoisted to protect an infamous traffic; and if it was never hoisted except as it is now hoisted on the coast of China, we should recoil from its sight with horror." And Gladstone's biographer, Lord Morley, writing years later, summed up his understanding of the nature of the war in the following words: "The Chinese question was of the simplest. British subjects insisted on smuggling opium into China in the teeth of Chinese law. The British agent on the spot began war against China for protecting herself against these malpractices. There was no pretence that China was in the wrong, for, in fact, the British Government had sent out orders that the opium smugglers should not be shielded; but the orders arrived too late, and, war having begun, Great Britain felt compelled to see it through, with the result that China was compelled to open four ports, to cede Hongkong, and to pay an indemnity of six hundred thousand pounds."

Sir George Staunton, an eminent Chinese scholar, in the British House of Commons, on April 14, 1843, said: "I have never denied that if there had been no opium smuggling, there would have been no war. Even if the opium habit had been permitted to run its natural course, if it had not received an extraordinary impulse from the measures taken by the East India Company to promote the growth, which almost quadrupled the supply, I believe it never would have created that extraordinary alarm in the Chinese authorities which betrayed them into the adoption of a sort of *coup d'état* for its suppression."

No mention was made of opium in the Treaty of Nanking [which terminated the war in 1842] and, therefore, the importation of the drug into China remained illegal under the Chinese law. By a treaty supplementary to that of Nanking, signed a year later, the British Government pledged itself to discourage the smuggling. This pledge was, however, almost immediately broken, and Hong Kong became a base of operations for the contraband trade in opium. The production and exportation of opium from India, prepared for the Chinese trade, continued to increase, and by 1858, arose to nearly 75,000 chests a year. As a further facilitation to this illegal trade, a British ordinance was passed which enabled Chinese boats, many of which were engaged in this trade, to fly the British flag, and out of this permission arose the "Arrow" incident which led to the second war between Great Britain and China.[1]

During the years immediately following the Opium War the British Government made repeated efforts to induce the Chinese authorities to legitimize the importation of opium into its borders. Lord Palmerston, in 1843, instructed the British representative in China "to endeavor to make some arrangement with the Chinese Government for the admission of opium into China, as an article of lawful commerce"; and advised [the first governor of Hong Kong] Sir Henry Pottinger, that he should "avail himself of every possible opportunity strongly to impress upon the Chinese plenipotentiary . . . . how much it would be for the interest of that Government to legalize the trade."

## The Chinese Government Succumbs

Despite the financial temptation to follow this advice, the Government of China for years refused to take this step. To one of the suggestions that he should do so the Chinese Emperor returned the following reply: "It is true that I cannot prevent the introduction of the poison; gainseeking and corrupt men will,

---

1. The *Arrow* was a ship owned by a Chinese resident of Hong Kong that was registered with the British authorities there. Chinese officers boarded the ship searching for a notorious pirate without British permission. The officers hauled down the British flag, provoking a shooting war.

for profit and sensuality, defeat my wishes; but nothing will induce me to derive a revenue from the vice and misery of my people." However, when it became clear that the smuggling of opium into China upon a large scale with the real, if not acknowledged, support of the British authorities, could not be prevented, and there was certainty that China would become involved in further serious disputes with foreign traders should she continue her attempts to punish opium smugglers, the Chinese Government, in 1858, reluctantly abandoned its fight to exclude the drug. The official British report, giving an account of the negotiations that were in progress upon this point said: "China still retains her objection to the use of the drug on moral grounds, but the present generation of smokers, at all events, must and will have opium. To deter the uninitiated from becoming smokers, China would propose a very high duty, but, as opposition was naturally to be expected from us in that case, it should be made as moderate as possible." The British negotiator suggested a duty from 15 to 20 taels a chest [a tael is equivalent to 1.2 ounces of gold]; the Chinese desired that 60 taels should be imposed in order that the duty might have some prohibitive effect. It was finally agreed that 30 taels should be collected, and thus as [historian Joshua] Roundtree says in his excellent volume *The Imperial Drug Trade*, "the drug which the Chinese Government has objected to so tenaciously for so long a time, and at such a costly price, now had its admission legalized at a less duty than England then levied on Chinese silks and teas." The result, thus finally achieved, Roundtree describes in the following words: "Great Britain had at last accomplished its desire, so long worked for, so little avowed. The Government of India was no longer to be the chief accomplice, the unsleeping partner of Chinese smugglers. The great drug trade was regularized by law. China had yielded to a steady continuous pressure, which it had not the strength to resist."

# Chinese Immigration Brings Opium Smoking to America in the Mid-1800s

*David T. Courtwright*

The Chinese began smoking opium in the seventeenth century. When Chinese peasants immigrated to the United States in the nineteenth century they brought the habit with them. In this selection David T. Courtwright explains that dissatisfied Chinese peasants left their homeland to become temporary sojourners to America during the 1848 California gold rush. The Chinese expected to earn money and eventually return to China. However, because they could not afford the travel expenses to America, the peasants became indentured laborers, bound to work off their travel debts. Feeling pressures such as these, Courtwright says, the Chinese laborers sought the comfort of practices that included opium smoking. Due to their extreme isolation, the Chinese workers were the sole opium smokers in the United States until around 1870. At this time some whites in the underworld began to experiment with the drug, and opium dens became popular with gamblers, prostitutes, and other criminals.

David Courtwright is a professor of history at the University of North Florida and the author of *Forces of Habit: Drugs and the Making of the Modern World* and *Violent Land: Single Men and Social Disorder from the Frontier to the Inner City.*

David T. Courtwright, *Dark Paradise*. Cambridge, MA: Harvard University Press, 2001. Copyright © 1982 by the President and Fellows of Harvard College. All rights reserved. Reproduced by permission.

The close association of the Chinese with opium smoking began well before the first wave of immigration to California. Opium was introduced into China by Arab traders around A.D. 700 and soon came to occupy an important place in the Chinese materia medica, much as it had in the West. Opium smoking, however, was not practiced until the seventeenth century. At first the drug was smoked in combination with tobacco, but sometime during the eighteenth century the tobacco was dropped and the opium smoked alone. It was not crude opium, but a refined product, of suitable strength, purity, and consistency for the pipe. How, where, and precisely when the boiling, evaporating, and straining processes for refining opium were developed is not known.

During the late eighteenth and early nineteenth centuries opium smoking was confined largely to the upper classes, especially to the idle young sons of wealthy families. But the practice soon spread to other classes, upward to the officers and belted gentry, and downward to the laborer and the tradesman, to the traveler, and [as writer Nathan Allen observed in 1850] "even to women, monks, nuns, and priests." Opium smoking also made great inroads in the army, undermining efficiency and morale. Jonathan Spence, an authority on opium smoking during the Ch'ing period, has speculated that different groups had different motives for smoking: eunuchs, members of the imperial clan, and soldiers took to the pipe to overcome their ennui; the wealthy, to relax and put aside their worries; the merchants, to increase their business acumen; and the laborers and peasants, to escape for a while the drudgery of their lives. Alcohol might have fulfilled these needs, as it did in the West; but the Chinese were rather moderate drinkers, so opium and tobacco emerged as the leading drugs.

## Revenue for the British

Another important factor was the eagerness of the British, who began exporting opium from India in the late eighteenth century, to sell large quantities to the Chinese. The opium traffic, although prohibited by imperial edict, was seen by the British as a lucrative source of revenue and a means of redressing an unfavorable balance of trade; conversely, responsible Chinese officials came to view the traffic as a source of domestic corruption and a serious drain on the nation's specie. Chinese efforts to end the illegal traffic, culminating in Commissioner Lin Tse-hsü's seizure and destruction of over 20,000 chests of opium stored in hulks off Lintin Island, provoked the series of skirmishes known as the First Opium War (1839–1842). Western weaponry and tactics prevailed; the Chinese agreed to pay a stiff indemnity, cede Hong Kong, and open five ports—Canton, Amoy, Foochow, Ningpo, and Shanghai—to foreign trade. From the standpoint of the opium traffic, the opening of these cities can be likened to the raising of five flood gates; the drug poured into the country in ever-increasing quantities. Another blow fell in 1858, when the Treaty of Tientsin effectively legalized the opium traffic. Imports nearly doubled, from 40,000 chests in 1839 to 76,000 chests in 1865. The spread of addiction, with the constantly increasing demand it entailed, also stimulated the domestic industry; cultivation of the opium poppy in China was widespread by the 1870s.

## Estimated Rate of Addiction

Assessments of the overall rate of addiction vary enormously. Depending on the estimated supply, the estimated average daily dose, the date the calculation was made, the region studied, and the political sympathics of the authority, anywhere from 1 out of 166 to 9 out of 10 Chinese were said to be addicted to smoking opium. In spite of the disparity of the estimates, one fact is clear: China maintained one of the highest rates of opiate addiction of any nation in the world throughout the nineteenth century. The immigrants who landed in California came from a society in which opium smoking was commonplace, the opium den an institution. Moreover, the overwhelming majority of immigrants came from the area around Canton, a region that had long been associated with the opium traffic, serving as the sole (though illegal) point of entry for the drug prior to 1842. Cantonese immigrants were especially likely to have knowledge of or actual experience with opium smoking.

## Many Chinese Decide to Emigrate

The Canton area, in addition to being a locus of the opium traffic, was in the mid–nineteenth century a region of profound turmoil. Political instability, widespread corruption, ethnic conflict, and population growth combined to put great pressure on the peasantry. Yet this pressure was matched by the peasant's determination to maintain his way of life; loyalty to family and clan were paramount. In the face of this conflict many Chinese resolved upon a course of temporary emigration. The idea was to work abroad, save as much as possible, and send money back to the family, with the ultimate goal of going back to China a wealthy and respected man. The embarking peasant's self-image was that of a sojourner, rather than a permanent emigrant, although relatively few who left managed to return to a life of ease.

The early sojourners found work in Southeast Asia, but with the discovery of gold in California in 1848, America's West Coast became the logical destination. The climate was amenable and cheap labor was badly needed to work the mines. The problem was how to finance the passage. Chinese merchants responded by devising a credit-ticket system, whereby the immigrant agreed to repay the cost of his passage, plus interest, through his labor in California. The debt repaid, the laborer could (at least in theory) accumulate enough money to sustain his family, buy a return ticket, and eventually retire to his homeland. But as long as he was in debt he was a virtual slave, forced to work where the merchant-creditor dictated and at the wages he stipulated. A network of "district companies," under the leadership of the merchants, evolved in California to ensure that the laborer up-held his end of the bargain.

## Chinatowns Emerge

It was an oppressive system, and the indentured laborer, bound to toil in an alien land until his debt was cleared, was subject to tremendous psychological pressure. To prevent that pressure from bursting into open revolt, some sort of safety valve was required. A leading historian of Chinese immigration, Gunther Barth, has suggested that the emotional safety valve was found in the early Chinatowns, especially in the vices they offered. (Chinatown, as Barth uses the term, refers to the Chinese quarter of any city or town, from San Francisco to the meanest mining camp.) The most popular forms of recreation were gambling, prostitution, and opium smoking, often found together in single or adjoining establishments. There the sojourner might lose his troubles in a game of fan-tan, in the company of a slave girl, or in the familiar fumes of smoking opium.

In addition to serving as a safety valve, this triad of vices served as a subtle means of reinforcing the debt bondage system. Gambling, prostitution, and opium smoking were expensive pastimes, particularly for steady customers. Opium smoking was notorious in this regard, because of its addictive potential. The indentured laborer who became addicted to smoking opium was literally on the slippery slope; he could make no headway repaying his original debt and soon acquired new ones. By the early 1880s the cost of an addict's daily supply of the drug was fifty cents or more, though the maximum daily income a Chinese laborer could hope to earn was little more than a dollar. Moreover, the time spent languishing in the den could not be used to earn income, a problem that worsened as the habit took deeper and deeper hold. The sense of despair the addict felt as the dream of returning to his homeland faded could only have increased his need for the soothing drug, creating a vicious circle of anxiety, opium smoking, more anxiety, and more opium smoking. Two groups benefited from the addicts' misery, the merchant-creditors and the secret criminal societies (tongs) that dominated the smoking opium traffic. The merchant-creditors retained control over the addicts' labor as long as their debts went unpaid, while the tongs fattened on the increasing consumption.

## Who Was Smoking Opium

There were several variations on this basic safety-valve pattern. Some Chinese immigrants were undoubtedly addicted, or had at least experimented with smoking opium, before they set foot in California. The most important evidence for this, aside from the high rate of addiction in China itself, is the fact that searches of arriving immigrants often netted concealed smoking opium. While the intercepted Chinese may have been doubling as couriers, as part of an organized smuggling operation, it is also possible that they were experienced users who had brought along a supply to tide them through the long sea voyage and the early uncertain weeks in the New World.

It is also possible that some of the resident merchant-creditors were or became addicted to smoking opium, although there is conflicting testimony on this point. Cortlandt St. John, an experienced New York opium broker, wrote in 1908 that "the better or merchant class of Chinese rarely use it." However, in 1870 William Speer, a missionary who instructed Chinese immigrants, complained that some of the brightest young merchants who entered his school fell victim to opium smoking, while San Francisco's health officer remarked that opium smoking was very general among the Chinese in that city, and not confined solely to the "loafing class." The merchant-smoker's higher income at least would have permitted him to avoid (or forestall) the pauperism that beset the common Chinese addict.

Finally, there was a type of user who might be designated a social smoker. He was not addicted, smoking only on occasion. Such recreational use of opiates without addiction was not unprecedented, but more Chinese opium smokers managed it than whites, especially whites who injected morphine. Perhaps this was because many Chinese understood opium smoking as something especially appropriate to holidays. Just as some American families imbibed wine only on sacred or festive occasions, these Chinese restricted their smoking to feast days, thereby minimizing the likelihood of physical dependence. They were also dealing with a somewhat milder drug; although opium prepared for smoking contained up to 9 percent morphine, when it was smoked only a fraction of the morphine was sublimated up the pipe. Most of it remained in the ash, or yenshee. Because less morphine was consumed, dependence took longer to develop—a full 15 days of regular smoking, according to one observer. This helped the occasional smoker escape full-blown addiction to the drug. . . .

## Opium Smoking by Whites

For 20 years, from roughly 1850 to 1870, opium smoking was confined to the Chinese. The principal reason the practice did not spread to whites during those years was the extreme isolation, physical and psychological, of the Chinese community. Since the typical immigrant saw himself as a sojourner, with no intention of settling, he had little incentive to abandon old ways and adapt to the new culture. Instead he banded together with his fellow sojourners, a tendency reinforced by the pooling of immigrants into labor gangs. The white community also contributed to this isolation. Ambivalence or outright hostility toward a strange race and their customs, coupled with a growing fear of cheap "coolie" labor, fueled a virulent anti-Chinese campaign, culminating in the 1882 Exclusion Act. Given their discordant goals and mutual distrust, Chinese and whites naturally avoided one another; they mingled, wrote political commentator James Bryce, "as little . . . as oil with water."

There was, however, one element of the white community

willing to mix with the Chinese: the underworld. Operating beyond the bounds of respectability, gamblers, prostitutes, and assorted other criminals would have had fewer scruples about associating with Asians or experimenting with their vices. The identities of the original white smokers are uncertain, although there are at least two apocryphal stories. The first, and most commonly quoted, was reported by [Doctor H.H.] Kane:

> The first white man who smoked opium in America is said to have been a sporting character, named Clendenyn. This was in California, in 1868. The second—induced to try it by the first—smoked in 1871. The practice spread rapidly and quietly among this class of gamblers and prostitutes.

A second account appears in a testimonial published by Dr. Samuel B. Collins, proprietor of an addiction cure. The letter, signed "Wm. L. Kennedy," begins

> Dear Sir:—I will probably reside in Kentucky this winter. You may use my name in your paper. I am known in all the large cities of the U.S. by most all OPIUM SMOKERS as I was one of the first who started use of the drug in the way of smoking it. That was in 1871, in the state of Nevada.

It is just possible that William Kennedy was the second smoker alluded to by Kane, as the two accounts agree on the 1871 date. It is also conceivable that there was no single chain of transmission, that the practice took hold in several different places at approximately the same time. In either instance opium smoking, once established, spread rapidly through the world of sporting characters in the 1870s.

## Why Smoking Opium Was Popular

The pipe's quick acceptance in the underworld poses some interesting questions. Why did so many gamblers, prostitutes, and other criminals take up smoking opium, in preference to some other opiate? The hypodermic injection of morphine was just becoming popular, and it was quicker, cheaper, and stronger. Moreover, prostitutes already had a history of opium and morphine use. Why should they not have continued as before?

The answer is twofold. In the first place, some gamblers and prostitutes continued to use opium and morphine, either because they happened not to be exposed to smoking opium or because they preferred the more traditional opiates. One who was addicted to opium or morphine in 1865 and had developed considerable tolerance might find it difficult in 1875 to switch to the milder smoking opium. But for members of the underworld who were not yet addicted, smoking opium possessed certain charms that opium or morphine lacked. Above all, opium smoking was a social vice, a way of relaxing and indulging with friends. "The morphinist wishes to be alone to enjoy his drug," explained Thomas Crothers, but the opium smoker "wants company, is talkative, his mind turns in a philosophical direction, to monosyllabic comments on men and events. He goes to a 'joint,' or a room which persons of a similar desire frequent." Inhaling the vapors of burning opium he is "immediately at peace with every one." Kane agreed with this assessment, declaring, "I have never seen a smoker who found pleasure in using the drug at home and alone, no matter how complete his outfit [pipe and paraphernalia], or how excellent his opium."

## Smoking the Opium Pipe

In many respects it was the nature and complexity of opium smoking that ensured its status as a social, rather than a private, act. Smoking opium, unlike tobacco or marijuana, cannot be stuffed into an ordinary pipe and lit; a special pipe and method of preparation are required. The opium pipe typically consists of a 16-inch to 20-inch bamboo stem, with a ceramic bowl inserted about a third of the way down from the stoppered end. Also required is some sort of lamp (as a source of heat), a large needle (to manipulate the viscous drug), and a knife (to scrape the bowl). The smoker, reclining on a wooden platform, dips the needle into a container of prepared opium, usually purchased from the proprietor of the den. He then holds the globule of opium above the lamp's flame, where it swells and bubbles to several times its original size. Once it is properly "cooked" and distended, the opium is transferred to the pipe's bowl, where it is rolled into a small "pill." This pill is forced into the hole at the center of the bowl and heated, then the needle stuck through and withdrawn, leaving a ring of smoking opium around the hole connecting to the pipe stem. The pipe is tilted, the flame heats the opium, and the smoker draws in the fumes. Then the whole process begins again, until the desired state is achieved.

Such a complex procedure must obviously be learned; it is not nearly so simple as downing a spoonful of Scotch Oats Essence or sticking a needle in one's arm. The neophyte who visited a den out of curiosity or at the urging of an associate was not unlike a student attending school; he was totally dependent on the experienced smokers for instruction. Once he mastered the art, he might in turn assume the role of instructor and transmit the ritual to others. All of this would have been impossible in isolation. Had smokers been as scattered and as secretive as morphine addicts, the practice would have died out in a single generation.

## The Opium Den Was a Sanctuary

An opium den (or "dive" or "joint") was more than a school, however; it was also a meeting place, a sanctuary, and a vagabonds' inn. Members of the underworld could gather there in relative safety, to enjoy a smoke with their friends and associates. One addict has left us a memorable portrait of life in the New York City dens. "The people who frequent these places," he recounted, "are, with very few exceptions, thieves, sharpers and sporting men, and a few bad actors; the women, without exception, are immoral." In spite of the desperate character of the clientele, fights were practically unknown. Instead, the smokers passed the time between pipes by chatting, smoking tobacco, telling stories, cracking jokes, or even singing in low voices. They might venture out for a bite to eat and return for some sleep. Early in the morning the prostitutes who worked the nearby neighborhoods would begin drifting in, to have a smoke before retiring. Even those who did not smoke would sometimes stop by to visit their acquaintances. Within the den a rigid code of honor prevailed: smokers would not take advantage of other smokers, or tolerate those who did. "I have seen men and women come in the joints while under the influence of liquor," continued the New York addict, "lie down and go to sleep with jewelry exposed and money in their pockets, but no one would ever think of disturbing anything." "The joint," confirmed an experienced Denver smoker, "is considered a sacred sanctum, and to betray . . . any conversation between the fiends is considered an unpardonable offense, and a fiend who commits a second offense of this character is generally debarred from all the rights and privileges of the joint."

## A Den in Every Major City

Another advantage, from the underworld point of view, was that there was a den in every major city, and practically every western town. "It's a poor town now-a-days," remarked a white smoker in 1883, "that has not a Chinese laundry, and nearly every one of these has its lay-out [pipe plus accessories]. You once get the first ticket [letter of introduction written in Chinese] and you're booked straight through. I tell you it's a great system for the fiends who travel." Availability was an important consideration, since many smokers, especially gamblers and prostitutes, pursued itinerant professions. Given all these advantages—comraderie, security, and availability— it is not surprising that the opium den became such a popular underworld institution during the 1870s.

# Physicians Abuse Morphine in the Late 1800s

*Thomas D. Crothers*

In 1900 a physician named Thomas D. Crothers wrote an article discussing morphinism, or health disorders caused by the addiction to morphine. Crothers believed that approximately 10 percent of all physicians at the time were self-administering morphine by injection. He called these doctors "morphinomaniacs" and said that the drug caused them to experience wide mood swings. The addicted doctors also tended to become manic and suicidal. Although the doctors tried to hide their use of morphine, Crothers said they were eventually discovered due to their childish display of egotism and their neglect of duty.

Thomas D. Crothers was a physician and a professor of nervous and mental diseases at the New York School of Clinical Medicine. He is the author of *Morphinism and Narcomanias from Other Drugs.*

In a general history of 3,244 physicians residing in the Eastern, Middle and some of the cities of the Western States, 21 per cent were found using spirits or opium to excess. Six per cent of this number used morphine openly. Ten per cent were using opium or other drugs secretly outside of this number. At least 20 per cent, including this number, used spirits in moderation,

Thomas D. Crothers, "Morphinism Among Physicians," *Current Literature*, vol. 27, January 1900, p. 45.

so called. In another study of 170 physicians, 7 per cent used opium or morphia, and 6 per cent were secret drug takers. From the personal observations of a number of physicians who have a large acquaintance with medical men, from 8 to 10 per cent are either secret or open drug and morphine habitués. These figures appear to be approximately correct, and show that at least from 6 to 10 per cent of all medical men are opium inebriates. This is undoubtedly a conservative statement, considering the fact that drug takers, and physicians in particular, are secretive and conceal their use of drugs, particularly where it implies weakness and reflects on their social standing. There are many reasons for the support of the statement of Dr. Elain that a large percentage of physicians die from drug treatment of themselves. They begin to use spirits, opium and other drugs for functional and transient disturbances, and later contract serious organic diseases, the early drug-taking having been a contributory cause.

## Characteristics of Morphinomania

Morphinism among physicians is usually associated with the use of this drug by the needle. The physician who uses opium is always somnolent, serene and meditative in his manner. The morphinomaniac shows great extremes of emotion. At times he will be very talkative and sensitive to his surroundings; then silent and indifferent. He will also at times be very brilliant, make a clear diagnosis, perform a difficult operation, and even deliver a lecture with spirit and energy. Morphinomania tends toward acute mania and suicide, with the impending danger from inflammations. There is a pleasing fascination in the rapid and complete change and transition which follows the use of the needle. To the psychopath, inherited or acquired, this is a revelation, and no other form of administering morphia can be compared with it. Thus [he] actually develops a needle mania, and nearly all morphinists are hypodermatic drug maniacs. The withdrawal of the morphia is unnoticed as long as the needle is used. In a certain case a physician used the needle with water, supposing it to be morphia, for two years after the withdrawal of the drug, under the direction of his partner. It has been stated, with some basis of fact, that the constant administration of drugs by the needle, and particularly morphia, is a prominent symptom of a morphinomaniac physician.

## Physicians Cannot Hide Their Habit

The medical morphinist may succeed in concealing his use of morphia for a variable time, but its effects on his thoughts and conduct cannot long be covered. He will early begin to show carelessness in conduct, neglect of duty, loss of personal respect, and emotional changes. Along with these appear a childish egotism, and a disposition to criticise and to expose the weaknesses of others. A recent example of this was the sudden slanderous disposition manifested by a quiet physician who was previously reticent as to the faults of others. For two years he created a good deal of bad feeling by his foolish criticisms and falsehoods. He was arrested for slander, and his morphinism was discovered.

# Opium Smuggling in India in the Nineteenth Century

*Charles Edward Buckland*

The following selection, written in 1892 by Charles Edward Buckland, is an account of the various methods opium smugglers used in nineteenth-century India. Buckland explains that one form of fraud was illicit poppy cultivation. Farmers secretly extended the borders of their government-licensed poppy fields to obtain higher yields of opium. The growers sold the excess opium at higher prices by shipping it out of town on trains. To avoid detection by railway police, Buckland says, smugglers resorted to throwing the opium packages out of train windows at night to those waiting to receive them. Another method smugglers used was to pack opium onto boats, carefully covering the drugs with onions, tobacco, or goatskins to mask the opium's strong odor. Detectives often caught these smugglers, however, by paying off informants. Buckland says that very little smuggling still took place in India at the end of the nineteenth century. Charles Edward Buckland is the British author of the *Dictionary of Indian Biography*.

Opium-smuggling, when it was first talked about in England, meant the forcible or clandestine introduction of opium into China. The former kind of opium-smuggling in China is now almost a thing of the past. The regular importers of opium no

Charles Edward Buckland, "Opium-Smuggling in India," *Blackwood's Edinburgh Magazine*, vol. 151, May 1892, pp. 669–77.

longer try to run a cargo by night in native lorchas or piratical junks. They find it more expedient to take the opium to the Custom-house, and to pay the duty that the Chinese Government discreetly levies on it. But opium-smuggling, in several different forms, has at times prevailed in India, where the poppy is cultivated and the opium is manufactured. Smuggling, as every one knows, depends chiefly on the difference between the natural and the artificial price of an article, be it whisky, or tea, or tobacco, or opium. Where, for the sake of the public revenue, an artificial price or value has been created, by excise laws or any other legislation, the smuggler comes in, and tries to make a profit for himself on the natural price of the goods. . . .

As the cultivation of tobacco is prohibited in England except under a special license from the excise authorities, so the cultivation of the poppy in British India is forbidden unless a license has been taken out. When a cultivator takes out a license from the Opium Department to cultivate a certain area (usually two-thirds of an acre of his own land), he receives an advance in money to secure his allegiance, and he binds himself to deliver to the opium agent, at a fixed price, ordinarily of 5s. [shillings] a-pound, whatever opium may be produced on his land. When official supervision is efficient, it is certainly very difficult for a man to cultivate poppy on a larger area than is covered by his license without detection. The cultivation cannot be concealed. It is a sort of a garden cultivation, the poppy-plants being grown in little squares or beds intersected by tiny water-channels for irrigation, wherever this is possible. The growth of the plants is carefully tended; and at length the time comes when they burst out into flower, and the fields look like a sheet of silver as the white petals of the flowers glisten in the morning dew. These beautiful petals are the first produce of the crop; for the women and children of the cultivators' families come forth and pick them off one by one, and carefully dry them, so that they may serve afterwards as the covering of the manufactured cakes of opium. Then the poppies, with their bare capsule-heads, remain standing in the open field, until it is considered that they are ripe for lancing. The cultivators then come forth in the evening, and, with an implement not unlike the knives of a cupping instrument, they scarify the capsule on its sides with deep incisions, so that the juice may exude. In the early morning the cultivators reappear with a scraping-knife and their earthenware pots, and they scrape off the exuded juice and collect it in their pots. And this is crude opium. It is obvious that cultivation carried on in this open manner cannot be hidden. If one man were disposed to have a little illicit cultivation on his own account, it would become known to all the village. Moreover, the native subordinates of the Opium Department and the English officer in charge of the district are frequently moving about, watching the progress of the crop, and vested with authority to measure the land if they suspect that either too small or too large an area has been cultivated. Still it seems quite possible that a man might so craftily amplify his boundaries that he might be cultivating a quarter of an acre more than he was licensed to cultivate. *Prima facie*, the produce of that extra quarter of an acre would become his own property, and he would be able to dispose of it by selling it to the professional smuggler. Perhaps it will be sufficient to acquiesce in the conclusion of the Commissioners that illicit cultivation is a thing of the past. There remains the fact that the cultivators, if they are dishonest, sometimes find themselves in the possession of a larger quantity of opium than they deem it expedient to deliver up to the Government opium agent. If this is so, they have to league themselves with the professional smugglers. The Government opium agent will pay them only 5s. a-pound for their opium. The smuggler can usually afford to pay them much more.

## Honest Poppy Growers Are Well Treated

There is, however, considerable inducement offered to the honest cultivator of the poppy not to smuggle. If he deals fairly and truly with Government, he has little to complain of. The estimated full produce of opium from an acre of poppy-land is 36 lb. weight. The price of this quantity at 5s. a-pound is £9 an acre. Out of this sum he will have received an advance in money of about £3, so that he has another £6 to receive when his opium has all been weighed in and tested. Very elaborate precautions are taken on both sides that there may be no cheating. The opium officials have to be careful that there are no little stones, or bits of mud, or other weighty but undesirable substances, mixed up under the mass of opium that looks like a lump of consolidated treacle [molasses]. At a later stage the official analyst, an English chemist, will ascertain if inferior sorts of opium have been mixed and covered up under an exterior of the best opium—though it is said that the experienced native testers can discover this by touch and sight almost as accurately as the analytical chemist. The cultivator, on the other hand, is usually present to see his pot of opium weighed; and if he cannot come himself, he may appoint men in his confidence to represent him, and to receive for him the ticket on which the weight and value of his produce are noted, with a view to the payment of the balance due to him. It is one of the marvels of India—which the hurried cold-weather Indian globe-trotters never behold—to see the crowds of opium cultivators assembled on one of the hottest days in the end of April, thousands and thousands of them, with their earthenware pots of opium, whilst one pale-faced English officer sits patiently under a large umbrella, from early dawn to late at night, watching the scales in which the pots of opium are weighed, and noting their contents and value in English in his book, as a check on the native accountants, who keep their books in the vernacular. The same officer is also careful to see that each man is paid the sum due to him, and it very rarely happens that any cultivator goes away discontented.

The bulk of the cultivators are certainly honest and content in their dealings. But let it be supposed that the men of a certain village have determined, or have been persuaded, to act dishonestly, so that they have kept back part of their produce, which they now intend to dispose of, for their own advantage, at a higher price than the 5s. a-pound that they would have obtained from the opium agent. There are two plain methods in which this may be done. There are certain shops licensed by the excise authorities for the retail vend of medical opium in every district. These shops are only kept open to prevent the people from having an excuse for using illicit opium. The shopkeeper binds himself to buy from Government as much excise or medical opium as will make it profitable to keep the shop, if he acts honestly; but he usually takes only the minimum quantity that he may consider sufficient to give a colour for keeping his shop open. The opium that he has to buy of the Excise Department is prepared in a form and colour differing much from the crude opium that he can buy from a dishonest cultivator; so that when the shopkeeper buys the illicit crude produce of a cultivator, he runs a considerable risk of detection—for, if he has a domiciliary visit from an excise inspector who examines his stock of opium, he ought certainly to be found out. Fortunately for him, subordinate excise officials are venal, and can close their eyes if the palms of their hands are properly tickled. But there is always the risk of a visitation from some native officer of higher rank and pay, or from an English official, who will be incorruptible.

## Smuggling on the Railway

The other method of disposing of the illicit opium is to sell it to some enterprising individual, who undertakes to collect a considerable quantity, and to send it down to Calcutta, or to the French settlement at Chandernagore, where it can be kept in safety until an opportunity is found for shipping it to China and the Straits, or for disposing of it to the Chinese residents in the capital. Before the East Indian Railway was carried through the heart of the districts in which the poppy is cultivated, the illict opium used to be sent down to Calcutta, sometimes in convenient parcels that a man could carry on his back, but more commonly by the country boats that navigate the rivers Ganges and Hooghly from Benares to Calcutta. When the railway was opened the smugglers soon took advantage of it. A man with a large package, ostensibly of onions, secured in a covering of goat-skin, took his seat at Patna in a third-class carriage, with his package under the seat, and in a few hours he and his opium arrived safely at Chandernagore or Calcutta, where he was welcomed by confederates.

In order to stop this kind of smuggling, the Government pays a very high reward, far in excess of the actual value of the opium, to any one who can detect and capture an opium-smuggler. Consequently, when a special railway police was organised, it soon came to pass that when the train arrived at the terminus for Calcutta several seizures were affected. The trains that arrived in the dark were usually patronised by the smugglers, and when the smuggler pulled out his package from under the carriage-seat, and stepped out on the station platform, he found himself accosted by some inquisitive policeman who wanted to know what was contained in the strong-smelling goat-skin package. The smuggler would probably offer a small sum of money to be let go, but that was of little avail, for there were other railway policemen looking on. It may be explained that as opium has a strong and peculiar odour, the smuggler tried to conceal it by packing it with onions, and in a full-flavoured goat-skin. But the railway police soon learned to distinguish this special combination of smells, and a constable with a good nose could wind it at times before the door of the railway compartment was opened. The detected smuggler was apprehended, and carried before a Calcutta magistrate and convicted. The men thus captured usually gave false names and addresses; but in some cases where their real name and the name of the village from which they came were discovered, measures were taken by the heads of the Opium Department to capture the rest of the local gang before they had time to learn the fate that had befallen their unlucky confederate.

## Throwing Opium Packages Out the Window

The smugglers became alarmed at the captures that were thus made in Calcutta, and for a time they tried the plan of throwing their packages of smuggled opium out of the windows of the railway carriages as the train passed along the borders of the French territory at Chandernagore. This could easily be done in the dark, and the confederates who were expecting the packages were ready waiting to carry them off into the French settlement. But there was a very clever and active officer at the head of the Hooghly district, where the boundaries of British and French territory meet, and as soon as he got wind of this new arrangement, he took measures to circumvent it. Although the French police in Chandernagore had the reputation of being in the habit of giving their protection to smugglers and other delinquents who could afford to pay for it, they had one great merit, for they were reasonable men and open to practical persuasion. If the smuggler paid 10s. to a French officer for protection, it was always possible, with the high rewards given for the detection of smuggled opium, to outbid the smuggler. If a detective of the British Excise Department offered 15s. to the French police officer, the latter saw the force of the argument, and the pitiful fellow who had only paid 10s. was betrayed into the hands of the English Philistines. The smugglers found that this form of conveying opium into French territory was not safe, and, at least for a time, they abandoned it.

But there was still a chance of working the goods department of the railway, and in one or two large consignments of rice that were made from Benares and Patna, the smugglers managed to introduce some bags that contained a quantity of opium well surrounded by grain. But this plan did not answer. Respectable consignors and consignees of grain were strongly adverse to it. Whilst the grain was lying at the warehouse of the railway station awaiting delivery to the consignee, the smell of the opium would assert itself and betray its own secret. Moreover, some of the confederates were obliged to run a great personal risk by going to the warehouse to try and rescue the particular bags that contained opium; and after one or two failures, followed by convictions of the smugglers, this plan was dropped.

## Smuggling by Boat

There remained the old plan of sending down the smuggled opium by country-boat, carefully packed and concealed under a cargo of onions, or tobacco, or hides, or anything that could mask or qualify the smell of the opium. A country-boat takes at least three weeks on its voyage downstream from Patna to Calcutta, even when the river is in full flood. The stream is very strong, but there is generally a high wind against the stream, and the wind catches the upper part of the boat, which in size and shape is very like a floating hay-stack, so that the boatmen have often to come ashore and take to the tow-rope and *tow down-stream* in order to make any progress. Meanwhile the consignment of this smuggled opium becomes known to too many individuals, some of whom have no inclination to keep a secret, especially when a shrewd detective officer is tempting them with a good round sum to betray it. There is a place called Sahebgunge on the river Ganges, halfway between Patna and Calcutta, where all the country-boats are required to stop to give particulars of their tonnage and cargo. This detention is for purely statistical purposes, according to the theory of the late Sir George Campbell, who introduced it; but it tends to the great personal profit of the native subordinates, who have the power to stop, and to let go, each boat as it passes. This was a favourite spot for the excise detectives, who could easily spot the smuggler with his cargo of onions and hides, beneath which packets of opium were concealed. The detectives or informers never attempted to stop or to seize the boat and its cargo at this point, for reasons which are obvious. They only took care to identify the boat and to ascertain to what place it was bound, and to whom the cargo was consigned. This could easily be ascertained from the papers which the captain or the supercargo of the crew was required to show for statistical purposes.

## Nepalese Smuggling

Of course the circumstances of each seizure of contraband opium differed more or less, but a description of one case will stand for many others. One great source of supply of contraband opium is in Nepal. The kingdom of Nepal is independent, and where its boundaries touch those of the British territory the Nepalese ryots [farmers] are in the habit of cultivating the poppy without any licence or interference from their own Government. There is a departmental rule under which any Nepalese ryot can take the opium that he has manufactured, and receive for it the price of 5s. a-pound from the nearest opium agency of the British Government; but as there is a chance of making a much higher profit for himself by selling it to some other person, the Nepalese ryot often adopts this course, and the purchaser from him becomes the smuggler, who has to get the opium thus obtained through British territory to the port of Calcutta. It was in May 1870 that sun old river-trader named Ram Dass found himself in possession of about 10 cwt. [½ ton] of opium that he had bought piecemeal from Nepalese ryots at an average of 7s. a-pound. This opium was collected on the Nepalese side of the river Gogra, and it was carefully packed and stowed away on board a large country-boat, under a cargo of timber and hides and onions. There was a crew of ten men to the boat, and Ram Dass, with his servant, travelled as supercargo. The boat's papers were made out as coming from Fyzabad, in the province of Oude, and the cargo was consigned to a native merchant at the large mart of Bhudressur, which adjoins the French territory at Chandernagore. The boat made a good passage down the Ganges. It was stopped and inspected (for statistical purposes only) at Sahebgunge, and at last the boat anchored off the town of Hooghly, waiting only for the turn of the tide to make its way in a few hours to Bhudressur. Ram Dass was considering himself a happy and successful smuggler.

## Capturing the Smugglers

But unfortunately for Ram Dass, he had enemies and rivals in his own country. He had declined to give a share in the spoil as hush-money to one of his brethren, and as soon as the boat with its freight had started on its journey, this individual went off and gave information to the nearest excise officer. The detective officers were soon set in motion; and by the time that Ram Dass and his boat had reached Sahebgunge (to be stopped there for statistical purposes) his coming had been anticipated, and he had been carefully identified and marked down for seizure on his arrival at Hooghly. Unknown to Ram Dass, the progress of his boat was further watched and reported from certain other points, and by the time that he arrived at Hooghly the officers of the Excise and Detective Department were ready to receive him.

When Ram Dass's boat dropped its anchor near the riverbank, off the old native fort at Hooghly, the rain was falling heavily, as it does rain in torrents in Bengal in July and August, and the crew were glad to shelter themselves under the thatched roof of the boat. Presently a voice from shore hailed them with the usual call, "Heh, Nayah!" (for every boatman is called Nayah or Noah, after the old admiral of the ark,) and some friendly advice was tendered as to the insecurity of the position that the boat had taken up. The boatmen were warned that the bore, or tidal wave, might upset them, unless they ran out a rope fore and aft to the shore to straighten the boat, and in compliance with this advice two stout ropes were carried out from the bow and the stern, and secured to strong posts in the river-bank. The crew having thus contributed to their own capture, the men on the shore departed for the night; but in the early morning an English sahib with several of his subordinates appeared, and asked Ram Dass for permission to go on board his boat. This permission being refused, they obtained the services of a passing fishing-boat and boarded the smuggler. Ram Dass and his men protested loudly, and threatened all manner of legal proceedings; but they were quietly told that their boat would be unloaded down to its bottom boards. "You may unload it yourselves," said Ram Dass; and then the boat having been hauled in close to the river-bank, the English officer and his men set to work to clear out the odoriferous cargo of onions and hides and timber. They toiled for several hours in the hot and steamy atmosphere, with alternate rain and sunshine, Ram Dass and his men looking on, and occasionally taunting them at their slowness—for Ram Dass still had hopes. He thought at least the sahib would want to go away and get some food, and then he might make a bargain with the native officials and be allowed to make away with the opium; but, to his dismay, another sahib and another batch of men came down and continued the work, and Ram Dass felt that the discovery of his opium was imminent. So he quietly got out over the stern of his boat into the river, hoping to swim away unperceived; but his manœuvre was noticed, and he was captured and brought back. Then the sahibs knew that it was all right; and at last they came upon the bags of opium, which were hidden under the cargo. Poor Ram Dass and his men were made prisoners, prosecuted, and convicted. Their boat confiscated, so also was the opium, on which a reward was paid to the informers and seizers that made them rich men for a time. The only men who got no immediate reward were the English sahibs, who were not allowed to take any money; but their reward came to them afterwards in the form of promotion and increase of pay, which they had so well merited.

I may conclude by telling one story of smuggling opium in

which an English lady was concerned. It happened many years ago, and all the parties concerned have long since gone to another world. It came about in this way. Mrs X. was the wife of a gentleman who was an indigo-planter at a factory not very far distant from the Nepalese frontier. It came to the notice of Mrs X. that every year, when her husband's indigo was being packed in chests to be forwarded to the Calcutta market, her *khansamah*, or butler, was very busy in collecting all the old jam-pots and pickle-jars, which he packed in an old indigo-chest, that was consigned to one of his friends in the Calcutta market. The *khansamah*, on being questioned, said that there was no sale for the old jars and jam-pots at the factory, so he tried to make a little profit out of them by sending them down to be sold in Calcutta, getting a free passage for them with his master's indigo. The lady's curiosity being aroused, she soon contrived to find out that the jam-pots did not go empty, but that they were filled with Nepalese opium, which could be sold for a good price to the Chinese dealers in Calcutta. A stone jar that had held 3 lb. of jam might be filled with the same quantity of opium that would be worth 30s. in Calcutta. The indigo season had been bad and unprofitable, and money was very scarce at the factory, so the lady determined to go into partnership with the *khansamah* in his opium speculation. After several anxious weeks of doubt and expectation, she was delighted to find that, as the result of their first joint venture, they had each realised more than 100 rupees, or £10 sterling. Subsequently she took her husband into her confidence, and when his poverty induced him to consent to a renewal of operations, his agents in Calcutta were rather surprised by the large indents for English jams in 3-lb. stone jars that they received from Mr X.'s factory. The jams, with the other factory stores, were sent up according to order, and months rolled on without any notice being taken. Meanwhile the lady and her *khansamah* had been busy in buying as much opium as they could get from the Nepalese cultivators, and at the same time the cook of the establishment was employed in making a considerable quantity of Tapari or Cape-gooseberry jam. The lady and the *khansamah* then proceed to fill about three-fourths of each stone jar with opium, whilst on the top of the opium was placed a layer of jam, and the lady, with her own fair hands, wrote out the English labels that were placed conspicuously on each jam-pot to indicate that the contents were of an edible character. Several indigo-chests were thus filled with jars containing opium below and jam above, and the lady expected to make a considerable profit for herself and her partner. But, alas! "The best-laid schemes o'mice and men Gang aft a-gley [oft do go awry]."

## Betrayed by an Ex-Employee

She had forgotten that one of her female servants, who had been lately dismissed, had become aware of her smuggling experiments, and this woman, out of revenge, went and gave information to the excise authorities, who pounced on the bullock-cart on which the chests were loaded before it had travelled half-way from the factory to the river, where they would have been safely put on board a boat with the indigo of the season. There was a considerable local scandal, and a severe penalty was levied on the unfortunate Mr X., who had to bear the responsibility of his wife's proceedings. I have never heard of any other similar attempt by a lady to smuggle opium. It only shows how difficult it is for the person who wants to evade the law, and run a cargo of anything contraband, to make sure that he has no private enemy who, for the sake of revenge, will give information to the excise authorities, and, in most cases, receive for himself the handsome reward that Government allows to the informers in order to protect its opium revenue. As a rule, however, there is now very little opium-smuggling, at least in the Lower Bengal province of India.

# CHAPTER TWO

# Opiates in the Twentieth Century

# Early Opiate Legislation

*John Kaplan*

Before the nineteenth century authorities made few attempts at opium prevention because opiate use was seen only as a personal weakness rather than as a social problem. In this selection John Kaplan outlines the history of early opiate legislation, explaining that the first major American narcotics legislation was passed in 1875 in San Francisco to shut down opium dens. Kaplan says that this legislation was in response to the anti-Chinese sentiments of whites who resented the Chinese for competing with them for railroad jobs. Because the opium smoking supposedly provided extra energy and ability to withstand hardship, it was thought that the Chinese had an unfair advantage. One of the results of this and further antiopiate legislation was an increase in illegal opium smoking. However, Kaplan explains that opium smoking accounted for only a small percentage of those addicted to opiates. Most addicts were southern, white, middle-class women who regularly took opiate tonics and were unaware of their addiction.

In 1914 Congress passed the Harrison Act that outlined the U.S. narcotics policy. The Harrison Act made it illegal to import, sell, or possess opiates except for medical purposes. Kaplan argues that opiate addiction has become a greater social problem since the enactment of the Harrison Act because once opium became illegal, its price skyrocketed and it began to be sold on the black market by criminals. Most addicts could no longer afford the drug without resorting to crime themselves.

John Kaplan, *The Hardest Drug*. Chicago: University of Chicago Press, 1983. Copyright © 1983 by John Kaplan. All rights reserved. Reproduced by permission.

John Kaplan is a professor of law at Stanford Law School in Stanford, California. He is the author of *Marijuana—The New Prohibition, Criminal Justice,* and *The Court-Martial of the Kaohsiung Defendants.*

Vigorous attempts to prevent opiate use are of restively recent origin. It has long been known that opium is addicting, but, until the nineteenth century, use of the drug was conceived of as a personal weakness rather than a social problem.

## Concerns About Opium in China

Probably the first nation to become concerned with the social consequences of opium use was Imperial China. During the eighteenth and nineteenth centuries, Chinese exports—tea, pottery, silks and the like—were enormously prized in Europe. Because China was virtually self-sufficient and needed few of Europe's products, it demanded payment for its goods in gold and silver. European merchants and their governments, as a result, searched for some way to ease their growing and frightening imbalance of trade.

In the latter part of the eighteenth century, the British discovered a sizable market in China for Indian-grown opium, and gradually encouraged the production and shipment of more and more of that drug. The Chinese authorities soon became alarmed, although not primarily on public health grounds. It is true that opium smoking was regarded as a vice, very much as cigarette smoking is today (or was until the Surgeon General's report of 1963 put the matter on a much firmer public health foundation). However, the Chinese government worried primarily about the increasing drain on their foreign exchange.

It was this concern that moved China to attempt to shut off opium importation—an effort which, as every student of colonial history knows, led to the Opium War of 1840–41. There it was decided by force of arms that China could not prevent the

Western nations from paying for its goods with opium.

Chinese imports of opium rose from 340 tons per year during 1811–21 to 6,500 tons in 1880. Domestic consumption increased even faster, since in the 1860s China attempted to save its foreign exchange by repealing its own ban on opium cultivation. Over the same period, missionaries, many of whom were American, began to protest the opium trade on grounds of morals, public health, and Chinese sovereignty. Although their campaign against Western shipment of opium into China was discernible much earlier, it did not attract much support in the United States until after the Spanish-American War.

In 1898, with the annexation of the Philippines, the United States for the first time acquired an Asian colony. Opium, there, was regarded as both a social and a health problem, and the American public began increasingly to listen to the sermons on the evils of the international opium trade.

## Civil War Morphine Addicts

The United States had had its own problems with opiates before this, though the public did not connect them with the international opium trade. During the Civil War, the relatively new drug, morphine, injected by the still more novel hypodermic syringe, was used—promiscuously by today's medical standards—to treat large numbers of battlefield injuries. As a result, after the war, the nation was left with a sizable population of morphine addicts. This problem, however, was treated almost exclusively as medical in nature—yet another kind of war injury. Morphine, the drug which not only caused but also alleviated the symptoms of the addiction, remained freely available.

The next major development in the American awareness of opiates came in the wake of one of the nation's recurrent racial problems. The Chinese coolies, who in the 1860s had been brought to build the western railroads, stayed on to compete with white Americans for jobs. Perhaps because of this, a series of unpleasant practices were ascribed to them, and their smoking of the exotic drug opium received a considerable share of the attention.

## First Major American Legislation

The prohibition of opium smoking had several attractions for those caught up in the anti-Chinese feeling. It stigmatized a practice associated with that despised minority. Insofar as opium provided the Chinese with their energy and ability to tolerate hardship (a very different view of the drug's effects than is generally held today), its prohibition was seen as depriving the aliens of an unfair advantage over American workmen. Finally, many hoped that the Chinese, deprived of access to their drug in the United States, might simply go back to China.

The first major American legislation in the narcotics field was responsive to the resentment against the Chinese. Beginning with a San Francisco ordinance of 1875 forbidding the keeping of opium dens, prohibitions on opium smoking were gradually adopted and extended in one western state after another. Congress joined in as well, raising the tariff on smoking-opium (a prepared, relatively mild form of the drug) in 1883; prohibiting the importation of such opium by Chinese in 1887; and prohibiting completely its importation in 1909.

The effect of these laws has never been investigated carefully. It has, however, been argued that their two principal consequences were to shift use to the still-legal morphine from smoking-opium, and to create a class of illegal opium smokers among those who clung to the use of that drug.

## Campaigns Against Opium Continue

Although the stridency of the campaigns against opium smoking continued to grow, the general outlines of our present narcotics policy were laid down in the Harrison Act of 1914, in response to quite different pressures. Because China had been the leading target of American missionaries, we had developed a unique relationship with that country, in which religious groups were far more vocal, and perhaps even more powerful, than commercial interests. Because of the missionaries' agitation against the opium trade, the United States had taken a major part in the international negotiations which resulted in The Hague Convention of 1912, outlawing the international nonmedical opium traffic.

It was realized then that the United States itself, apart from its restrictions on smoking opium, exercised virtually no comprehensive control of its own internal traffic. Opium smoking was a relatively minor cause of opiate addiction here, but "tonics" and patent medicines were virtually unregulated, and many contained opiates. It was said that the largest group of addicts consisted of southern white women who did not even know they were addicted. They knew only that their "tonic," taken regularly, prevented the sickly feeling that came on whenever they missed their medicine. Obviously this situation was inconsistent with a major thrust of the Progressive movement. Patent medicines containing morphine or opium were dangerous, and it was the function of government to protect the consumer from harmful foods and drugs. It is perhaps no coincidence that the Harrison Act was passed approximately midway between the Pure Food and Drug Act (1906) and Prohibition (1920).

## Physicians Argue Against Patent Medicines

Finally, the rise of the medical profession also played a part. Just around the turn of the century, physicians began upgrading their profession. More stringent educational and licensing requirements became part of this as knowledge of physiology and medicine expanded, until according to one authority: "Somewhere between 1910 and 1912 in this country, a random patient, with a random disease, consulting a doctor chosen at random, had for the first time in the history of mankind, a better than fifty-fifty chance of profiting from the encounter." Patent medicines were a major competitor of professional medical treatment, and in the physician's view, a most inferior one. As a result, the American Medical Association campaigned vigorously for the prohibition of opiates outside of medical channels.

## The Harrison Act

In any event, the Harrison Act of 1914 made illegal the importation, sale, or possession of opiates except within medical channels. Such drugs could be obtained legally only if pursuant to a physician's prescription, and pharmacists were required to keep detailed records to prevent diversion.

Even more important than the Harrison Act itself were its implementing policies and regulations. The language of the statute could be read either as permitting a physician to prescribe narcotics to fulfill an addict's need or as forbidding this practice. The legal issue involved the interpretation of an exception to the general prohibition on the supply of opiates. Such drugs might be prescribed by a physician "in the course of his professional practice and where said drugs are dispensed or administered to the patient for legitimate medical purposes," and the question was whether this language permitted the physician to prescribe opiates solely to prevent his patient's going through withdrawal. The authorities enforcing the law immediately took the position that the language of the Harrison Act did not comprehend mere maintenance of addicts on opiates, and began prosecutions of physicians who acted according to a contrary interpretation.

## Prescriptions for Opiate Addicts Are Forbidden

The first case reaching the U.S. Supreme Court affirmed the validity of these prosecutions, and although the Court later changed its mind about the meaning of the Harrison Act, the American policy forbidding prescription of opiates to maintain addicts had already been firmly laid down. From then on, it was enforced by medical associations, state laws, threats of federal prosecution, and a whole range of governmental and nongovernmental sanctions; nor was it disputed by the vast majority of medical practitioners, who regarded narcotics addicts as extremely difficult and unsatisfying patients.

The effect of this was not only to eliminate the "scrip doctors" who promiscuously gave out prescriptions for opiates, but also to deter those who would have maintained addicts under careful medical supervision. For a while, the authorities tolerated, indeed encouraged, the organization of specialized clinics out of the control of individual private practitioners to maintain addicts on opiates. Gradually, however, even these were closed down.

It is by no means clear even today whether this occurred because of abuses that cropped up in the clinics or because the federal authorities held to a generally prohibitionist philosophy. In any event, by 1923, with the closing of the last remaining maintenance clinic (in Shreveport, Louisiana) there were no legitimate sources of opiates for maintaining addicts.

From then until the 1960s, the national narcotics policy changed only in the direction of progressive increases in the penalty structure. Indeed, the only significant modifications made since have been the repeal of certain mandatory minimum sentences and the allowance, under many restrictions, of methadone maintenance.

## The Effects of the Harrison Act

The consequences of sixty years of opiate prohibition are subject to some dispute. Several facts are clear, however. First, the type of addict has changed dramatically from the pre–Harrison Act days. Then, opiate addicts tended to be middle-class and middle-aged women from rural areas or small towns. They took their morphine or opium orally and certainly were not regarded as particularly criminal—though their use was not without problems, as pictured in [playwright] Eugene O'Neil's autobiographical *Long Day's Journey into Night*.

Within fifteen years after the passage of the Harrison Act, the addict was much more likely to be male, urban, lower-class, and young. He was typically an injector of heroin, and regarded as a serious criminal problem not only with respect to the violations of the drug laws inherent in using a prohibited substance but with respect to property crimes as well.

A considerable part of this transition can be explained by the change in the legal treatment of opiates. Because of the difficulties of smuggling and concealment, more potent opiates such as heroin became favored over morphine and—even more so—over opium. Similarly, injection grew to be favored over drinking in a "tonic" because of the greater effectiveness of the former means of administration per milligram of opiate.

Because all their legitimate sources of opiates had been cut off, those who remained addicted could receive drugs only from criminals. To derive social support for their use, to maintain their supply, and to avoid detection, they were forced to join a comparatively tight, drug-using subculture. Since opiate users were already stigmatized and in close contact with criminals, opiates themselves acquired a criminal meaning and their use came to be seen as a way of defying the mores of the wider society.

## Opiates Became a Greater Social Problem

Finally, the price of opiates had increased so enormously that to sustain a habit required considerably more than many addicts could earn through honest work. This was especially so since the search for a continuous drug supply consumed a great deal of their time and effort.

There are those who assert that these changes are outweighed by the likelihood that the percentage of opiate addicts in the population has been markedly reduced since the Harrison Act. Though this is probable, it is by no means certain, since the estimates of the number of addicts before 1914 are even less reliable than our data as to the number today. Moreover, even if addicts constituted a higher percentage of the population before 1914 than today, addiction was then so much less personally destructive and socially costly that the balance is clear. It is hard to deny that opiates have become a far greater social problem since the passage of the Harrison Act.

# Doctors Prescribe Heroin in the Early 1900s

*Arnold S. Trebach*

In this selection Arnold S. Trebach describes the development of heroin in a chemistry lab and its early uses in medical treatments. Trebach notes that the compound chemist C.R. Alder Wright produced in his lab in 1874 remained nearly unknown until German pharmacologist Heinrich Dreser popularized the drug twenty-four years later. Dreser named the drug heroin, from the German *heroisch*, meaning strong, powerful, or heroic. Dreser believed heroin was a more effective and safe treatment for respiratory problems than morphine and codeine. In an era before the development of antibiotics, when respiratory diseases were the leading cause of death in some countries, heroin became a "miracle medicine," used widely in many countries. Trebach points out that the fact that heroin was first used medically dispels the ongoing myth that the drug was initially used as a treatment for morphine addiction.

Although many doctors were at first enthusiastic about heroin, medical reports began surfacing about its addictiveness. Heroin soon replaced morphine as the drug of choice on the streets of eastern American cities. Trebach says that reports at the time exaggerated the extent of heroin abuse and that some politicians deliberately presented it as a major national problem when it was not.

Arnold S. Trebach is president of the International Anti-

Arnold S. Trebach, *The Heroin Solution*. New Haven, CT: Yale University Press, 1982. Copyright © 1982 by Yale University. Reproduced by permission of the author.

Prohibitionist League and was the founder and president of the Drug Policy Foundation, a leading international drug policy organization. He has worked as a university professor, writer, civil rights advocate, and creator and leader of nonprofit and entrepreneurial enterprises. Trebach is the author of *The Rationing of Justice, The Great Drug War, Legalize It? Debating American Drug Policy* and editor of *Drugs, Crime, and Politics*. He has coauthored numerous other books, including *Strategies for Change: New Directions in Drug Policy, New Frontiers in Drug Policy, The Great Issues of Drug Policy, Drug Prohibition and the Conscience of Nations,* and *Drug Policy 1989–1990: A Reformer's Catalogue.*

In a report in the coldly scientific pages of the *Journal of the Chemical Society*, published in 1874 by Harrison and Sons, Printers in Ordinary to Her Majesty, St. Martin's Lane, London, chemist C.R. Alder Wright described a series of experiments he had conducted to determine the effect of combining various acids with morphine. History has not provided us with a clue as to why he did so or what he was looking for. In any event, during the process of experimentation he boiled a sample of morphine with acetic anhydride, a chemical related to ordinary table vinegar, and produced a long list of compounds, including, among others, one that later became known as heroin or, more scientifically, as diacetylmorphine or diamorphine.

At the time the world did not beat a path to chemist Wright's door. Indeed, he did not seem to believe that his discovery was of any major significance, and most accounts today . . . do not even give him credit for it. That glory has usually been reserved for the man who both named this relatively new medicine (from the German *heroisch*—strong, powerful, or heroic) and popularized it, some twenty-four years after Wright's article appeared. German pharmacologist Heinrich Dreser reported on his experiments at the Elberfeld facility of Friedrich Bayer and Co. in a paper he read in 1898 to the seventieth congress of German naturalists and physicians. By modern standards the report was an eloquent, even highly personal, endorsement of a then relatively unknown drug for the treatment of coughs, chest pains, and the discomfort of pneumonia and tuberculosis. (This was of more than academic medical interest in the late nineteenth century, since antibiotics were not yet known. As Dr. Musto has observed, "In the United States . . . tuberculosis and pneumonia were the two leading causes of death. Understandably, pharmaceutical research concentrated on treatment of respiratory diseases and their symptoms.") Dr. Dreser told his scientific and medical colleagues in Dusseldorf, "This diacetylester of morphine, called 'heroin' showed a . . . strong . . . sedative effect on respiration when compared with morphine." Moreover, Dr. Dreser claimed, heroin was much safer to use than other drugs, such as codeine, because "for heroin the lethal dose is a hundredfold higher than its effective dose, while for codeine the lethal dose is only tenfold higher than its effective dose." In other words, Dreser believed, it was difficult for a doctor to prescribe a fatal overdose because a small dose of heroin provided therapeutic relief so rapidly.

## A Physician's Endorsement of Heroin

The accompanying report by a Dr. Floret provided even more revealing insights into how the drug was used during the last century in actual clinical experiments with human beings, including, in this case, the physician himself. Dr. Floret wrote:

> For six months I have been prescribing heroin . . . to patients of the walk in clinic of the Farbenfabriken of Elberfeld. Heroin proved to be an extremely useful, prompt acting and reliable drug in treating persistent coughs as well as chest pains which resulted from inflammation of both the upper and lower respiratory tract. . . . Approximately 60 patients have been treated by me with this drug so far. They all agreed that they noticed an immediate improvement and relief from the persistent cough immediately after taking the powder. . . . They also observed that the pains associated with the cough

were reduced: "Doctor, the powder that you prescribed was indeed very good. Immediately after taking the powder I felt relief, I had to cough a lot less and in general the cough improved a great deal after taking the powder. . . ." I also had an opportunity to test the surprisingly fast and reliable effect of heroin on myself. A persistent hacking cough which was associated with an inflammation of the upper respiratory tract hindered my clinical activity considerably. Particularly the requirement for speaking resulted frequently in severe coughing attacks, which were immediately arrested by a single dose of 5 milligrams of heroin so that I could pursue my activities for many hours without being affected by coughs.

Thus we have the first widely known open endorsement of heroin, the miracle medicine. Some of the myths about it concern the work of Dreser and Floret. Even the authoritative tome *The Opium Problem*, published in 1928 by Dr. Charles Terry and Mildred Pellens, dealt with the discovery of heroin as a "most unfortunate influence" and observed, in a misleading passage, "Dreser in Germany in 1898 produced heroin . . . which was put out as a safe preparation free from addiction-forming properties, possessing many of the virtues and none of the dangers of morphin and codein, and recommended even as an agent of value in the treatment of chronic intoxication to these drugs." Such half-truths were repeated and increasingly distorted over the years; a typical version presented in 1974 in an otherwise sound book by John B. Williams, *Narcotics and Drug Dependence*, claimed: "Heroin was first produced commercially in Germany in 1898 by Dreser as a cure for morphinism."

## The Persistence of a Myth

But as we have seen, Dreser and Floret viewed heroin as cough, chest, and lung medicine. While they believed it to be nonaddictive, in this report neither doctor advocated the use of heroin in the treatment of morphine addiction. Nevertheless, the mythological explanation of heroin's birth is widely accepted even today by leading academicians and drug-abuse officials. Dr. John C. Kramer, of the Department of Medical Pharmacology and Therapeutics, University of California at Irvine, was sufficiently intrigued by the persistence of this myth to conduct an investigation of it. He reported in 1977 that "between 1899 and 1902, four physicians, a German [not Dreser], two Frenchmen, and an American, wrote papers advocating the use of heroin as an aid in withdrawal from morphine addiction." But even these four physicians were quite cautious about the use of heroin in addiction treatment and generally did not advocate long-term maintenance with the drug. Dr. Kramer wondered, as have I, about how the myth started. His answer:

> In the years following 1910, Hamilton Wright [a prominent physician, antinarcotic crusader, and statesman] and others sought to push the nation and Congress to support narcotic control legislation. In part they did this by exaggerating certain data and distorting reports regarding addiction. Among the myths they created was the depiction of all opiates as the "Demon Flower." . . . In particular, heroin was painted as a special evil. The frequency of its use as a substitute in withdrawal was exaggerated far out of proportion to the facts and the statement that it had been first introduced for this purpose was totally false. Not only was the tale used as a means to demonize heroin but it also offered an opportunity to unfairly depict physicians as important contributors to the drug problem. Evidently, the story was not contradicted at the time and thus became part of popular belief. Repeated in print over the years, even authorities in the field have come to accept it as valid. The bad press that heroin received during the late teens and the twenties was unjustified.

Kramer emphasized that the story that heroin was "introduced . . . as a substitute in the treatment of morphine addiction" was a "totally erroneous belief."

## Medical Use of Heroin Spread Rapidly

It would seem, nevertheless, that the medical world must have been waiting for a new narcotic drug for the treatment of organic illnesses—one that might be nonaddictive. Dreser's report was published in the Berlin *Therapeutic Monthly* in September 1898. His speech was mentioned in the November issue of the *Journal of the American Medical Association*. The December 3, 1898, edition of the *Lancet*, the leading medical journal in England, told of a new preparation: "It is said to be a favorable substitute for morphine by not altering the blood-pressure and thus to be well borne by persons of a weak heart and feeble arterial system. Heroin is also said to be free from other disagreeable secondary effects of morphine, so that it may be administered in respiratory diseases . . . in comparatively large doses with no effect but that of a sedative upon the air passages. These statements are so promising as to render desirable a careful clinical trial of this new derivative in this country."

I have encountered no evidence of such *careful* clinical trials in England or elsewhere. But there is evidence that heroin spread rapidly throughout the medical establishments of many countries within the first few years after Dreser's speech. The Bayer company advertised the new drug in a number of languages—German, Italian, Russian, and English, among others. The ads for heroin often included another famous compound from the Bayer laboratories, named by Dreser in the year after his heroin speech—aspirin. But most of the medical interest remained in the more powerful narcotic drugs. As the turn of the century approached, a wide range of such opiates became available: the venerable opium itself, codeine (the other principal active ingredient in opium, although much weaker than its more powerful relatives), morphine (the more powerful essence of opium), and heroin (which in layman's terms we might call the essence of morphine). While all these opiates had general painkilling qualities for such conditions as terminal cancer, the medical reports at the time seemed to emphasize the original purpose set out by Dreser and Floret—control of the discomfort of the then-widespread scourge of tuberculosis and related conditions.

The reports on heroin in the treatment of such conditions

were often enthusiastic. For example, another German physician, H. Leo, related the case of a 71-year-old man suffering from severe coughs and shortness of breath. He was hospitalized, then sent to a special sanitarium and given a standard array of drugs. Even so, his condition deteriorated, respiration became more labored, and his heart action was poor. By February 1899 the man was in agony, in a constant state of fear, and unable to sleep at night. Then, on the evening of February 3, 1899, heroin was given to him. Dr. Leo wrote: "February 4. . . . After he had taken the drug he felt very comfortable and stated he no longer felt sick. The action of the heart was somewhat more regular. The appetite was better. February 5. . . . The sensation of fear that was always with him was gone. . . . The cough was without difficulty. February 6. . . . The action of the heart was regular. The heroin was then withdrawn for eight days. The ailments he had suffered before gradually returned. Heroin was again administered and had the same beneficial action as before."

## Heroin Has Addictive Danger

But other doctors soon gave evidence of the sad fact that, alas, there is no Garden of Eden on this earth, at least not one without serpents and prices to pay for the pleasures, or even simple human comforts, gained. The medical literature began to contain reports of the addictive danger of this new drug, which many had hoped would have the relief-giving powers of the other opiates but without the constant danger of addiction. (No such narcotic drug has ever been found.) In 1902 Dr. Morel-Lavallé, who advocated the use of heroin in treating morphinism and considered heroin generally safer to use than morphine, still felt compelled to warn his colleagues about the habit-forming potential of heroin. And Dr. G.E. Pettey was moved to write an article for the *Alabama Medical Journal* in 1903 entitled "The Heroin Habit Another Curse," in which he declared that of the last 150 people he had treated for drug addiction, eight were dependent on heroin, and three of these had started their habit on that drug. In Dr. Pettey's experience, heroin dependence was just as difficult to cure as the more common addiction to morphine.

Despite many such cautionary reports, the clinical popularity of heroin was widespread during the first decade of this century. In 1911 Dr. J.D. Trawick wrote in the *Kentucky Medical Journal:* "I feel that bringing charges against heroin is almost like questioning the fidelity of a good friend. I have used it with good results, and I have gotten some bad results, such as a peculiar band-like feeling around the head, dizziness, etc., but in some cases referred to, it has been almost uniformly satisfactory." However, Dr. Trawick's balanced approval of the medicine, and that of many other of his colleagues, was not to prevail.

## Heroin on the Streets

There is evidence that during the same year in which Dr. Trawick's article appeared heroin abuse started to increase rapidly in New York City. Heroin soon replaced morphine as the drug of choice among the youthful recreational users on the streets of several large Eastern cities. Reports on annual admissions for heroin and morphine addiction to Bellevue Hospital during this period, assembled by Dr. W.A. Bloedorn and brought to recent attention by David Musto, reveal that the first admission for heroin addiction was made in 1910, that one being the total for the year, compared with 25 for morphine addiction. By 1914 it was 149 heroin to 398 morphine. By 1915 the balance had swung to 425 admissions for heroin addiction compared with 265 for morphine.

By 1917, for reasons not completely clear, the movement had begun in earnest to transform heroin abuse from a troubling personal vice into a major national problem. During the rapid enlargement of the armed forces in 1917, rumors began to spread about the huge number of addicts in the service. Representative Henry Rainey declared that 80,000 draftees had been found unfit for service because they were addicted to drugs. In 1918 Dr. Royal S. Copeland, health commissioner of New York City, estimated that there were 150,000 to 200,000 addicts in the metropolis, most of whom were dependent on heroin, and many of whom were "recently discharged soldiers" under twenty-five. Clearly there were large numbers of heroin addicts at the time, but there also seems no doubt that, then as now, estimates of the size and growth of the problem varied widely.

## The Number of Heroin Addicts Is Exaggerated

The reasons for the public attention to heroin are equally hard to divine. One plausible explanation is that America's entry into World War I signaled the start of a period of agonizing social stresses and tensions. It was, in a way, the end of a period of isolation and innocence and the beginning of an era of fears about foreign involvement, German atrocities, Communist conspiracies, and crime and violence in the city streets. As Dr. Musto observed in 1974, "The crucial factor in heroin's transformation does not seem to have been the incidence or character of heroin use in 1917, but rather the context in which the phenomenon was interpreted. In 1917, the United States harbored a climate of ambiguous fears, which coexisted with the nation's desire to react unanimously in order to preserve the world's freedom. The battle was not against an enemy of the United States, but the enemy of mankind." In this context it might have seemed acceptable to some officials, Musto reasoned, to deliberately exaggerate the number of heroin addicts and the danger they presented to society—so long as the result was greater unity among the citizenry in order to save America from a whole catalog of new threats. "The drug was one more convenient object on which to place the blame for social disorder."

# Heroin Abuse in the 1920s

*Lyman Beecher Stowe*

In the following selection Lyman Beecher Stowe describes the heroin addict of the late 1920s in New York City. Stowe views all heroin users as criminals or potential criminals. Indeed, Stowe reports that heroin is the favored drug of over 80 percent of the inmates in New York City prisons. Heroin, Stowe believes, leads the addict into a life of destruction and senseless cruelty. For example, the addict will pointlessly kill while he is robbing someone. Although many addicts are involved in the underworld, Stowe says, 34 percent are from the professional world. Most heroin addicts obtain the drug via international drug rings that are the major distributors in the United States, where most of the heroin that is smuggled in passes through New York City. Stowe says that international efforts to limit the production of opium products and to reduce the cultivation of opium poppies have been ineffective. Lyman Beecher Stowe (1880–1963) was a writer and the grandson of Harriet Beecher Stowe, the well-known author of *Uncle Tom's Cabin*.

A few years ago [late 1920s], Toughie Reed sat in a California jail waiting to be hanged. Still in his teens, he was a thief and a murderer—and, before either, a drug addict. And now he was describing how he had first been "hooked" by a dope peddler, in a San Francisco pool room.

"Then this guy comes up to me and says he's got something that'll give me a wonderful kick. 'Aw, go on,' I tells him,

Lyman Beecher Stowe, "Halo of Heroin," *Forum*, vol. 83, June 1930, pp. 346–50.

'I don't want your stuff.' But he keeps right on talking and telling me how fine it makes you feel, and then he says, 'You're a good sport, ain't you?' 'Yeah,' I says—'Sure I'm a good sport.' 'Well,' he says, 'a good sport'll try anything once, won't he? A good sport ain't afraid.' And he holds out something and says, 'Here—you can try a dose for nothing.'"

The boy was silent; he looked down at the white knuckles of his clenched hands.

"Jeeze, I didn't want anybody to say I wasn't a good sport. . . . And anyway I was sort of curious by that time. He was giving it to me free and he told me where I could find him if I wanted some more."

The hands relaxed helplessly and the knuckles were faintly flushed. He looked up.

"Jeeze, what could I do? . . ."

The rest of the story was obvious. When the first effect wore off, Toughie found that he craved more, went to the peddler, and got it. The desire recurred at more or less regular intervals and each time his wants were supplied free of charge. When he had become a slave to the habit, he found that the drug was no longer a gift, but was to be had only at an exorbitant price. Furthermore, nature had automatically entered into the conspiracy and had established a "tolerance" in his system which necessitated a constant increase in the doses in order to obtain the same reaction. This meant money—and Toughie had no money.

He became a robber and eventually a murderer; was arrested, imprisoned, tried, and sentenced to be hanged. He appealed to the governor for a pardon so that he might devote his life to warning other young people against drugs. Naturally the governor did not and could not pardon him. But even though addicts are notorious liars, there is no reason to doubt the youth's story. Its beginning and its end are only too representative of the well-known practice of this illicit traffic.

Respectable people are likely to think that the narcotic habit is an evil limited solely to the underworld and to the Orient. They deplore it, of course, but they merely shrug their shoulders: after all, these two worlds are far removed from theirs—the one socially and the other geographically. Yet recent revelations show that the high-powered drugs manufactured from the derivatives of opium are far more devastating than the smoking of opium itself is or ever was in the Orient, and also that no class in society is immune from these secret and sinister dangers.

Although authorities agree that all addicts are either criminals or potential criminals, one should not assume that the converse is equally true. John I. Cotter, whose positions as Secretary of the Court of Special Sessions of New York City and Secretary of the New York Narcotic Survey Committee give weight to his opinion, holds that no *first-class* criminal is or can be a slave to the habit. If such a criminal becomes an addict, he loses almost at once the physical and mental powers which brought him his infamous success. It is significant that dope peddlers are frequently their own best customers, whereas few, if any, of the men higher up—the brains of the traffic—ever touch the stuff. Certainly the Sherlock Holmes stories give a completely false picture. By no possibility could the great sleuth have retained his extraordinary abilities and still have been constantly crying, "Quick, Watson, the needle!"

## The Heroin Addict Becomes Senselessly Cruel

This is not to deny that the drug habit leads to an entire disregard of consequences—a brazenness which may be mistaken for cleverness and bravery. Heroin, the most powerful of the opium derivative drugs and, in New York at least, the most commonly used (it is the favorite of over eighty per cent of the addicts in New York prisons), is especially conducive to this foolhardiness; indeed, its name comes from the fact that it makes the taker feel heroic. The heroin addict becomes obsessed by a sense of exalted ego which leads him to the destruction of life and property. While under the temporary magic of the stimulant, he loses all fear of what may follow his often rash acts. He becomes senselessly cruel. If he robs a person, for instance, he will kill him without compunction—and frequently without necessity.

I might cite innumerable instances of this madness, but I believe the following two stories will illustrate the point. A few years ago a gangster named Louis Cohen—a drug addict— spied an enemy gangster seated in a car which was parked in front of a New York police station. Though it was broad daylight, and in spite of the presence of a group of officers a few paces away, Cohen whipped out his gun and killed the man. Exhibit B is the case of an addict (also a criminal) who was driving through Wichita, Kansas, and was stopped by a policeman for disregarding some traffic regulation; without warning, and apparently without cause, the man shot the officer dead.

Perhaps these two instances—and there are many more— may give some hint as to why crimes of violence have shown such a marked increase within the past decade [1920–1930], and why drug addicts form over forty per cent of the inmates (excluding persons jailed for petty offenses) of the prisons of New York City.

## Heroin Not Confined to Underworld

There are equally interesting statistics and case histories which tend to disprove the supposition that narcotic indulgence is confined to the underworld. In a [1930] study of 1563 drug addict cases, over thirty-four per cent were found to come from the professional classes. Personal narratives— some of which may seem incredible—also indicate that the evil knows no social distinctions.

An attractive young wife, the daughter of a professor in one of our leading Eastern universities, fell into the drug habit and took to pawning everything she could lay hands on in order to get money to satisfy her craving. Her husband would return from a business trip to find that she had pawned practically the entire contents of their apartment. He finally refused to continue living with her, and this shock apparently enabled her to discontinue dope and to attempt a reform. It was not

## THE HISTORY OF DRUGS

# Junkies and the Mafia

*In the beginning of the twentieth century, the Mafia became involved with the illegal use and distribution of heroin. It was at this time that the term "junky" was coined.*

The majority of heroin users in the USA at the beginning of the twentieth century were young, white, working-class men who took the drug for purely "recreational" reasons. Often they were gang members and taking heroin was part of the initiation process. It was in this era that the term "junky" first appeared—coined to describe addicts who stole junk metal to support their habit. The use of drugs for recreational purposes was nothing new, opium smoking had been growing throughout the West and was almost endemic in China at the time, but the almost immediate association of heroin with criminality was [new]. This association was to grow once those other bogeymen of the twentieth century—the Mafia—got involved.

### The Czar of Crime
In the early days, the illicit heroin business was run mainly by the Jewish gangs. Slang terms of Yiddish origin such as "schmecher" (an addict) and "smack" (heroin) testify to this connection. The Italians disapproved of both drugs and prostitution, preferring to stick to more "honourable" activities like the "numbers game" (gambling), the black market and, from 1920, bootlegging (illicit alcohol production). But Salvatore Lucania, aka Charles "Lucky" Luciano, changed all [that] . . . Luciano dragged the Mafia into the modern age and it is largely due to him that the link between the Mafia and drug trafficking was established.

Julian Durlacher, *Heroin: Its History and Lore*. London: Carlton, 2000, pp. 17, 20.

long, however, before she had succumbed again. This time, in company with a lover, she took to writing pleading letters to graduates of her father's university whereby she got several "loans." She and her companion were caught and they are now serving prison terms.

That a woman of culture and the best of training could so completely sacrifice to her appetite her home, husband, reputation, honesty, and even decency may appear—as I said—incredible. But it is true. It is merely a typical instance of the results of drug addiction. Similar cases could be recited almost without number.

## Impossible to Count Those Addicted

Since the drug habit is a secret vice, it is impossible to estimate accurately the number of addicts in the country. The reckonings vary all the way from one hundred thousand to several millions. That of Judge Collins of the Court of General Sessions in New York, one of the most conservative authorities, is 166,000 known addicts of whom ten thousand are in New York City. This estimate is more impressive if one realizes that addiction is a disease one of whose symptoms is an intense proselytizing zeal for converts. Such is the perversity of human nature under the influence of drugs that a man may loathe his habit and long to be rid of it, and yet at the same time will exercise the utmost ingenuity to involve those dearest to him in its toils. Thus a year or two ago a college Freshman became an addict and since then, impossible as it may seem, has converted his entire family—three brothers, two sisters, and father and mother—to the habit.

## Recruiting the Young

That the lad was so young when he first became an addict is typical of the narcotic situation. The ubiquitous agents of the great drug rings make a particular effort to gain recruits among young people. Ellen La Motte, one of the wisest and best-informed authorities on the drug problem, in her book, *The Ethics of Opium*, states that one-third of the addicts acquire the habit before they are twenty, and one-half before they are twenty-five. The technique of "hooking" greenhorns is, as with book agents, more or less definite. Usually it is similar to that described by the unfortunate Toughie Reed.

Where do these narcotics come from? Are they domestic or imported products? If the latter, how are they brought into this country? Perhaps the answers to these questions may point to an escape from the present conditions under which drug consumption is an increasing menace.

## The Sources

There are 8600 tons of opium produced a year, although three hundred tons are sufficient for medical and scientific purposes. The fifty drug factories of the world are located in Switzerland, Germany, Japan, France, Holland, England, and the United States. And in spite of international conventions and many national anti-narcotic laws, they are merrily turning out many times the amount of drug derivatives legitimately required. Because of our great wealth and population we are getting more than our share of this plentiful supply. Our per capita rate of drug consumption is, in fact, one of the highest in the world.

This is only to be expected. We are wealthy, and drug addiction is an expensive luxury both for the nation and for individual addicts. The average expenditure per day per addict is about five dollars, making an annual outlay per person of $1825. Thus, assuming that Judge Collins' estimate of 166,000 addicts is accurate, the total annual expenditure for narcotics in the United States is $302,950,000.

Stephen G. Porter, Chairman of the Foreign Affairs Committee of the House of Representatives and another authority on the drug menace, believes that the resultant annual economic loss to the country is a billion dollars. This includes loss of earning capacity, loss of property in holdups and robberies, the cost of the arrest and prosecution of dope peddlers and smugglers, and their maintenance in prisons and other institutions. (More than thirty-two per cent of the prisoners in the Federal penitentiaries have been sentenced for violating the narcotic laws.)

## Most Heroin Smuggled into the United States

Although the output of our own four drug factories increased between 1923 and 1928 from twenty-three and a half tons to seventy tons, under the innocuous supervision of the Federal Narcotics Control Board, nevertheless ninety per cent of the habit-forming drugs, such as opium and its derivatives—morphine, codein, heroin—and also cocaine, are smuggled into this country; and eighty-five per cent of this is smuggled through the port of New York. Almost every steamer brings drugs to our shores.

One could hardly imagine anything easier to smuggle than white dust. Fashionably dressed women conceal it on their elegant persons or among their effects. It affords them easy money in large amounts. But such persons are only retailers, as are the members of the crews, who hide drugs in all manner of places throughout the ships and then sneak them ashore after port has been reached. One device is to put the forbidden narcotics in the water tanks of life boats.

## International Drug Rings

The wholesale smugglers are the great international drug rings. They do business on a huge scale and supply the several drug rings now functioning within the country. Arnold Rothstein, the gambler who was murdered in a New York hotel in 1928, was the head of one of the latter organizations. Under the direction of the importers and the distributing agents, narcotics are furnished to peddlers who ply their trade in every city in the land.

Sometimes the smugglers are caught—sometimes not. Just as this article is being written the newspapers contain stories of a large shipment of drugs which was seized by inspectors after a great liner had docked in New York. In this instance, the contraband was concealed in a trunk, but the hiding places are sometimes more difficult to locate.

In 1926, a consignment of packing cases alleged to contain toys being shipped from Hamburg, Germany, to Kobe, Japan, reached New York Harbor. The customs officials were suspicious and had the goods trailed from the Manhattan dock to South Brooklyn, from which point they were to continue their journey to Japan. The truck stopped at a loft where the packing cases were unloaded and replaced by others apparently identical. At this point all hands were arrested. The cases which had been unloaded were found to contain one hundred and twelve pounds of morphine and two hundred and twenty-five pounds of heroin.

These drugs had probably cost less than five thousand dollars; the profit on their sale in the United States would have been close to one hundred thousand dollars. Assistant District Attorney Edward Silver prosecuted the case with such vigor and skill that, in spite of the powerful influence of the drug ring heads, he secured a ten-year prison term for the man directly responsible, eight years for the assistant in charge of the loft, and two years for the driver of the truck. The evidence in the case disclosed the fact that five similar shipments, on which profits were presumably in the neighborhood of half a million dollars, had come in undisturbed during the three preceding months.

## Anti-Narcotic Weapons

Without well-directed and unceasing effort, and also public enlightenment, little can be done to combat the drug menace. Fortunately, we have both to-day and in time shall have even more of each. One of the foremost leaders in the fight is Captain Richmond Pearson Hobson, who first came to the attention of the public as the man who sank the Merrimac and thus bottled up Santiago Harbor during the Spanish-American War. Captain Hobson organized the International Narcotic Education Association, of which he is president, and the World Conference on Narcotic Education, of which he is the secretary general. Both organizations are invaluable in the campaign against drugs.

An expert committee of the World Conference on Narcotic Education has, for example, made a study of the schoolbooks in which information on the effect of drugs and the drug traffic could be fittingly included and has prepared statements for insertion, with the approval of author and publisher, at appropriate points in the text.

These associations were the originators and sponsors of Narcotic Education Week during which an effort is made to unite the combined forces of the press, the pulpit, the platform, and the radio in warning the public against the drug menace. The fourth such week was observed last February [1930]. It was immediately preceded by a conference held in New York at which available information on the problem was presented, discussed, and referred to the proper committees. Resolutions of policy on the various narcotic measures now before our Congress or the Opium Advisory Committee of the League of Nations were presented.

## World Conference for Drug Control

Since the drug problem is essentially international, the associations are about to open an office in Geneva and are arranging a world conference to meet in London in 1931. The last meeting of the Assembly of the League of Nations instructed the Opium Advisory Committee of the League to call a conference to frame a convention for limiting the output of drug factories to the medical and scientific requirements of the world. This committee has had a curious and interesting history. Until recently it has been dominated by the delegates representing the principal drug-manufacturing nations—France, Japan, Holland, Switzerland, Germany, and last and most important, Great Britain. While under this domination the committee confined itself to gathering information about the constant increase in the manufacture and distribution of dangerous drugs and to passing resolutions expressing pious regrets and vague hopes that something might be done about the matter.

Then, in 1925, the American delegates, headed by Congressman Porter, becoming disgusted with this pious futility, left the convention and refused to have anything further to do with the League's opium activities. Shortly thereafter, some of the delegates representing non-drug-manufacturing countries, like Venezuela, China, and Italy, began to see the cloven hoof beneath the saintly cloak of their associates, to whom the drug business meant huge profits for fellow nationals and important government revenues. Almost 24 per cent of the colonial revenues of the British Empire in the Far East are derived from taxes on opium.

The delegates of the victimized nations—the nations in which drugs are sold but not made—have finally, under the leadership of His Excellency M. Cavazzoni of Italy, and the pressure of public opinion, caused the Assembly to instruct the Opium Committee to call this convention. The committee, however, is showing no impatience to set the date for the conference, and in the meantime the drug manufacturers are reaping their usual profits from the illicit traffic.

## Limiting Opium

The consensus of opinion among the disinterested students of the world's drug problem seems now to be focusing upon these two main objectives: first, the adoption of some enforceable plan which will limit the output of manufactured drugs to the world's legitimate medical and scientific needs; and second, the gradual reduction in the growth of the poppy from which opium is derived, and the coca leaf, the source of cocaine, to a similar basis. The authorities estimate that it will take at least twenty years to accomplish this limitation in growth, whereas the limitation in manufacture could be put into effect in a year.

Robert Underwood Johnson, former Ambassador to Italy, recently said to Captain Hobson, "Should it for any reason become necessary to discontinue all the efforts to improve human conditions except one, your anti-narcotic campaign is the one that should be continued." And the campaign *will* be continued. Its leaders are conducting it in the right fashion. They have their method and their goal. With the example of the prohibition blunder before them they are trying to avoid the error of having the law precede the public opinion essential to its enforcement.

# The CIA Allies with Asian Drug Warlords in the Mid–Twentieth Century

*Alfred W. McCoy*

In this selection Alfred W. McCoy describes how the Central Intelligence Agency (CIA) allied itself with drug warlords in Burma, Laos, and Afghanistan from the 1950s through the 1980s. The CIA made these alliances in order to gain the allegiance of tribal armies to fight Communist Soviet Union and China. The warlords, with CIA knowledge and support, increased their power by expanding local opium production and by smuggling heroin internationally. McCoy says that by 1971, 34 percent of all American soldiers in South Vietnam were addicted to heroin largely supplied by CIA allies. Furthermore, when the military market was saturated in Vietnam, heroin suppliers shipped the drug to the United States, where it became a large part of the illicit drug trade.

In the early 1980s the CIA formed new alliances with drug traffickers in Afghanistan to enlist their support in resisting the Soviets. Once again the opium and heroin trade grew. The CIA director at the time said that the CIA's main objective in Afghanistan was to fight the Soviets and that the agency did not have the resources or the time to investigate the drug trade.

Alfred W. McCoy is a professor of Southeast Asian history at the University of Wisconsin–Madison. He has written about Southeast Asian politics for more than twenty years and is the

Alfred W. McCoy, "Drug Fallout," *Progressive Magazine*, August 1997. Copyright © 1997 by Alfred W. McCoy. Reproduced by permission.

author of many books, including *The Politics of Heroin: The CIA Complicity in the Global Drug Trade, The Politics of Heroin in Southeast Asia*, and *War on Drugs: Studies in the Failure of U.S. Narcotics Policy.*

Throughout the forty years of the Cold War, the CIA joined with urban gangsters and rural warlords, many of them major drug dealers, to mount covert operations against communists around the globe. In one of history's accidents, the Iron Curtain fell along the border of the Asian opium zone, which stretches across 5,000 miles of mountains from Turkey to Thailand. In Burma during the 1950s, in Laos during the 1970s, and in Afghanistan during the 1980s, the CIA allied with highland warlords to mobilize tribal armies against the Soviet Union and China.

In each of these covert wars, Agency assets—local informants—used their alliance with the CIA to become major drug lords, expanding local opium production and shipping heroin to international markets, the United States included. Instead of stopping this drug dealing, the Agency tolerated it and, when necessary, blocked investigations. Since ruthless drug lords made effective anti-communist allies and opium amplified their power, CIA agents mounting delicate operations on their own, half a world from home, had no reason to complain. For the drug lords, it was an ideal arrangement. The CIA's major covert operations—often lasting a decade—provided them with de facto immunity within enforcement-free zones.

In Laos in the 1960s, the CIA battled local communists with a secret army of 30,000 Hmong—a tough highland tribe whose only cash crop was opium. A handful of CIA agents relied on tribal leaders to provide troops and Lao generals to protect their cover. When Hmong officers loaded opium on the CIA's proprietary carrier Air America, the Agency did nothing. And when the Lao army's commander, General Ouane Rattikone, opened what was probably the world's largest heroin laboratory, the Agency again failed to act.

"The past involvement of many of these officers in drugs is well known," the CIA's Inspector General said in a still-classified 1972 report, "yet their goodwill . . . considerably facilitates the military activities of Agency-supported irregulars."

Indeed, the CIA had a detailed knowledge of drug trafficking in the Golden Triangle—that remote, rugged corner of Southeast Asia where Burma, Thailand, and Laos converge. In June 1971, *The New York Times* published extracts from another CIA report identifying twenty-one opium refineries in the Golden Triangle and stating that the "most important are located in the areas around Tachilek, Burma; Ban Houei Sai and Nam Keung in Laos; and Mae Salong in Thailand." Three of these areas were controlled by CIA allies: Nam Keung by the chief of CIA mercenaries for northwestern Laos; Ban Houei Sai by the commander of the Royal Lao Army; and Mae Salong by the Nationalist Chinese forces who had fought for the Agency in Burma. The CIA stated that the Ban Houei Sai laboratory, which was owned by General Ouane, was "believed capable of processing 100 kilos of raw opium per day," or 3.6 tons of heroin a year—a vast output considering the total yearly U.S. consumption of heroin was then less than ten tons.

By 1971, 34 percent of all U.S. soldiers in South Vietnam were heroin addicts, according to a White House survey. There were more American heroin addicts in South Vietnam than in the entire United States—largely supplied from heroin laboratories operated by CIA allies, though the White House failed to acknowledge that unpleasant fact. Since there was no indigenous local market, Asian drug lords started shipping Golden Triangle heroin not consumed by the GIs to the United States, where it soon won a significant share of the illicit market.

# Narcotics in Afghanistan and Pakistan

Within a few years, the currents of global geopolitics then shifted in ways that pushed the CIA into new alliances with drug traffickers. In 1979, the Soviets invaded Afghanistan and the Sandinista revolution seized Nicaragua, prompting two CIA covert operations with some revealing similarities. During the 1980s, while the Soviets occupied Afghanistan, the CIA, working through Pakistan's Inter-Service Intelligence, spent some $2 billion to support the Afghan resistance. When the operation started in 1979, this region grew opium only for regional markets and produced no heroin. Within two years, however, the Pakistan-Afghanistan borderlands became the world's top heroin producer, supplying 60 percent of U.S. demand. In Pakistan, the heroin-addict population went from near zero in 1979 to 5,000 in 1981 and to 1.2 million by 1985—a much steeper rise than in any other nation.

CIA assets again controlled this heroin trade. As the Mujaheddin guerrillas seized territory inside Afghanistan, they ordered peasants to plant opium as a revolutionary tax. Across the border in Pakistan, Afghan leaders and local syndicates under the protection of Pakistan Intelligence operated hundreds of heroin laboratories. During this decade of wide-open drug-dealing, the U.S. Drug Enforcement Agency in Islamabad failed to instigate major seizures or arrests.

In May 1990, as the CIA operation was winding down, *The Washington Post* published a front-page expose charging that Gulbudin Hekmatar, the CIA's favored Afghan leader, was a major heroin manufacturer. The *Post* argued, in a manner similar to the *San Jose Mercury News*'s later report about the contras, that U.S. officials had refused to investigate charges of heroin dealing by its Afghan allies "because U.S. narcotics policy in Afghanistan has been subordinated to the war against Soviet influence there."

In 1995, the former CIA director of the Afghan operation, Charles Cogan, admitted the CIA had indeed sacrificed the drug war to fight the Cold War. "Our main mission was to do as much damage as possible to the Soviets. We didn't really have the resources or the time to devote to an investigation of the drug trade," he told an Australian television reporter. "I don't think that we need to apologize for this. Every situation has its fall-out. . . . There was fallout in terms of drugs, yes. But the main objective was accomplished. The Soviets left Afghanistan."

Again, distance and complexity insulated the CIA from any political fallout. Once the heroin left Pakistan's laboratories, the Sicilian mafia managed its export to the United States, and a chain of syndicate-controlled pizza parlors distributed the drugs to street gangs in American cities, according to reports by the Drug Enforcement Agency. Most ordinary Americans did not see the links between the CIA's alliance with Afghan drug lords, the pizza parlors, and the heroin on U.S. streets.

# The U.S. Heroin Epidemic in the 1960s and 1970s

*Robert L. DuPont*

The following article was written in 1974 by psychiatrist Robert L. DuPont. DuPont worked in the District of Columbia's Department of Corrections in the late 1960s and early 1970s. He reports that during this time, half of those incarcerated in Washington, D.C., prisons were heroin addicts. The city was in the throes of a heroin epidemic that lasted, according to DuPont, from 1966 to 1970. The majority of those addicted were born after World War II and were lower-class African American males. DuPont says that heroin use spread rapidly at this time. However, attitudes about the drug began changing early in the 1970s, when treatment programs were provided, the dangers of addiction were recognized, and the street price of heroin rose dramatically. DuPont says that the heroin epidemic hit almost all cities in America as well as other countries including Britain, France, and Germany.

Robert L. DuPont is a practicing psychiatrist who specializes in the prevention and treatment of addiction. He is also a professor of clinical psychiatry at Georgetown University Medical School in Washington, D.C., as well as senior vice president and medical director of Bensinger, DuPont and Associates, a company offering employee assistance programs and substance abuse intervention and prevention.

A major heroin epidemic is now receding [in 1974] in cities across the United States, leaving in its wake hundreds of thousands of addicts, as well as changed national attitudes toward crime, cities, and race. Since many of these attitudes are badly distorted and could have negative, long-term consequences, it is important to set the record straight on this complex subject.

My experience with the problems of heroin addiction grew out of my work as a psychiatrist with the District of Columbia Department of Corrections in 1967 and 1968. My colleagues and I found that of the 800 men committed to D.C. jails each month, about half were addicted to heroin; furthermore, addiction was a major cause of the crimes that led to their imprisonment. It was obvious that the prisons and community were offering little help to these people and that massive efforts would have to be made to solve the problem of heroin addiction. One aspect of this new effort was the creation in 1969 of a city treatment program, the Narcotics Treatment Administration (NTA), which I directed from its inception until 1973. During those four years NTA treated more than 15,000 people for heroin addiction.

## New Heroin Users

Analysis of NTA records tells much of the story of the heroin addiction epidemic. Among our findings were that an overwhelming number of the patients were new users of heroin and that nearly two-thirds began use between 1966 and 1970—the epidemic years. Even among those who came into treatment in 1973, few had begun using heroin after 1970. For example, 3,100 patients had started on heroin in 1969, but by 1973 the number had dropped to fewer than 100. At first we thought that new users were simply no longer coming to the center, but as we monitored the data, it became increasingly clear that the lag in seeking treatment accounted for only a small part of the decline.

We also found that heroin addiction in Washington did not occur randomly in the city's population. While it existed in virtually all segments of the population between the ages of ten and seventy, it was highly concentrated among lower-class, black young men.

The ethnic and economic composition of the addicted population was not unexpected, but we were surprised to find that more than half the people treated by NTA were born between 1945 and 1954—the years of the post–World War II baby boom. The severity of the epidemic among this relatively small segment of the population can hardly be exaggerated. Of the young men born in 1952—the peak birth year for heroin addicts—fully 20 percent became addicted to heroin and were subsequently cared for by the city's narcotics treatment program.

The attack rate, to use public health terminology, among those living in the poorer sections of the city was double the city-wide rate. For individuals born during the peak years it was more than fifty times greater than the rate for individuals born only ten years before, or a few years after, 1952.

In the last few years public concern has focused on heroin addiction among returning Vietnam veterans and on the spread of heroin addiction out of the ghettos and into the middle-class suburbs, but neither of these developments contributed more than a small fraction to the total addiction problem in Washington.

Another critical finding from the NTA experience was that the use of heroin spread rapidly from one new user to another during the epidemic. As one patient told me, "I began using heroin just like I began smoking cigarettes—right after my best friend started using it, he turned me on to it at a party in his home." Few within the susceptible group were acquainted with long-term addicts, and almost all were convinced that they themselves would not become addicted.

## Attitudes Change Toward Heroin

By 1970, however, this attitude had changed, and heroin was no longer regarded as casually as cigarette smoking. The devastating effects were all too clear—deaths due to overdoses and prison terms for using and selling heroin had become almost everyday occurrences.

The heroin scene changed dramatically in Washington as the epidemic peak passed. Overdose deaths, which rose to eighty-two in 1971, fell to seventeen in 1973—and only four of these occurred during the last six months of the year. In early 1972 more than 30 percent of the defendants arraigned in D.C. Superior Court tested positive for heroin. Today [1974] that

## THE HISTORY OF DRUGS

# Heroin Use During the Vietnam War

*Heroin addiction among soldiers during the Vietnam War was possibly the most serious disease epidemic in modern military history.*

When the first alarmed and exaggerated reports of the epidemic filtered back in 1970, it seemed that every young American in Vietnam was in danger of contracting the most frightening disease of our time—heroin addiction. At first, there was almost total confusion. Some commanders were slow to realize the seriousness of the problem. They denied that heroin use was spreading among the troops. A few journalists went to the other extreme, one reporting that as many as half the men in some units were using heroin.

While drug use among American troops never reached such staggering proportions, it did become perhaps the gravest disease epidemic in modern military history. To this day no one can say with pinpoint accuracy how many men became heroin users at the peak of the epidemic. The best estimate that we have, supported by chemical tests as well as by a Gallup poll of Vietnam veterans, is seven percent of Army enlisted men. If an epidemic were to reach such drastic levels in the population of the United States, 10 to 15 million victims would be involved.

Richard S. Wilbur, "How to Stamp Out a Heroin Epidemic—Army Style," *Today's Health,* July 1972.

number has fallen to fewer than 10 percent.

The number of patients peaked in July, 1972, when more than 4,700 people were in NTA treatment. By the spring of 1974 this number had fallen to less than 2,000. Significantly, the crime rate in the nation's capital, as in some other cities, has also dropped dramatically.

## Heroin Use Declines

How can we account for the decline in heroin use? First, the provision of treatment offered an alternative to the pusher's and street addict's life-style, and gave individuals a chance to rebuild their lives. Successful law enforcement efforts to diminish the supply of heroin also made a difference—in less than two years the street price of heroin in Washington rose from about $1.00 a milligram to more than $5.00.

Finally, and perhaps most importantly, among those in the susceptible population there was a growing awareness of the dangers of addiction, leading to the widespread rejection of heroin use. It is one thing to grow up knowing that there is an older fellow on the next block who is addicted to heroin and quite another to have many of your close friends either strung out, in jail, or dead from an overdose. It took several years for the more appalling consequences of heroin addiction to become obvious to susceptible youngsters, but once they were apparent, a cultural immunity developed.

## Future Outlook

What are the implications for the future? It is obvious that large numbers of people have become seriously addicted to heroin and that some of them will have problems for years to come. Treatment must continue to be available to the addicted. We must intensify efforts to reduce the supply of illicit drugs, just as we must continue to support those forces that reject heroin addiction in the community. Community acceptance of former addicts must be fostered so that we do not make permanent outcasts of thousands of people. Drug abuse trends must be closely monitored to spot potential epidemics early, and when the signs appear, vigorous intervention aimed at reducing the supply of the drug and at reducing the demand for the drug through prevention and treatment must take place before the epidemic rages out of control as it did in the late 1960s.

While we have been talking about the Washington experience, many American cities are now reporting similar, although less steep, downturns in heroin addiction. More remarkable than these downward trends is the realization that almost all American cities had a heroin epidemic at about the same time as Washington. The peak in new heroin use occurred as early as 1967 in some places—notably New York City and Los Angeles—and as late as 1971 in other cities, particularly smaller, inland ones. Thus, there was evidence of spread over time, but the range of epidemic peaks was narrow. Even more striking, epidemic peaks occurred at about the same time in many other countries. Britain, France, Germany, and even Hong Kong, to mention only a few, appear to have had similar epidemics. Cities and countries had vastly different levels of heroin use, but in most cases the number of new users reached a peak within the same period of time.

## Reasons for the Heroin Epidemic

This similarity in timing is not easy to explain. One is tempted to look for a correlated rise in other social problems, but poverty, crowding, racial prejudice, and unemployment—all possible explanations—did not suddenly peak in the late 1960s. In fact, at that time all these ills were showing modest improvements in Washington, as they were throughout most of the United States.

In part, the spread can be traced to the role of mass communications and mass travel. But it is in the new, epidemiological understanding of heroin addiction that we may find other and probably more revealing clues. Heroin addiction was concentrated among the people born after World War II. It occurred predominantly among the great bulge in the population, which, by sheer mass action, created the youth culture of the late 1960s. World War II and the subsequent rise in fertility rates were worldwide experiences—as were the youth culture, college demonstrations, and the heroin epidemic. Each of these events was itself serious and complex—I am not arguing that they were trivial or even that they sprang from similar roots. I am, however, arguing that they occurred more or less simultaneously and that changes in the structure of the population contributed to this timing.

# Asia's Golden Triangle Produces Heroin for Global Consumption

*Rodney Tasker*

Rodney Tasker reports in this selection that the Golden Triangle, which includes parts of Burma, Laos, and Thailand, had a bumper crop of opium in 1989. In Burma, the world's largest opium producer at the time, the United States had discontinued its antinarcotics aid. As a result, Burmese farmers returned to growing poppies and drug warlords increased their production of heroin, the semisynthetic narcotic drug made from opium. In Thailand, the main transit point for Golden Triangle drugs, the police and militaries from fourteen countries tried to keep the plentiful opium harvest from being smuggled out of the country, but with little success. Although opium was banned in Thailand in 1958, Tasker says, older-generation Thais continue to smoke the drug and use it as a painkiller and as a cooking seasoning. Laos has also become a major producer of opium, harvesting three hundred tons of the drug in 1989. Rodney Tasker is a British reporter and journalist for the *Far Eastern Economic Review*, a weekly Asian business magazine published in Hong Kong.

Rodney Tasker, "Seed of Destruction," *Far Eastern Economic Review*, vol. 146, November 23, 1989, pp. 46–47. Copyright © 1989 by the *Far Eastern Economic Review*. Reproduced by permission of Copyright Clearance Center, Inc.

The Golden Triangle has never seen a bumper crop of opium like the one harvested [in 1989] in Burma, Laos and Thailand. This record crop means that more heroin than ever is leaving the area for worldwide consumption and more heroin than ever can be found on the streets of Thailand. "If you can afford a beer, you can afford heroin here," was the way one foreign narcotics expert put it.

Despite the boost in supply, international street prices remain roughly the same, but the average purity of a "fix" has risen, and, in turn, so have the chances of an addict overdosing. Thailand, in addition to serving as the main transit point for the Golden Triangle, faces a serious domestic addiction problem—estimated by the United Nations International Narcotics Control Board to number about 300,000. With the bountiful supply, the purity of heroin for sale has risen to about 90% while the price has fallen. A unit of heroin, 700 g, can be bought for Baht 5,000 (US$193.42) in Bangkok, but it may cost up to US$1 million overseas. A social worker in Bangkok's slums estimates that a typical heroin addict would spend only Baht 80–140 a day.

## Stopping International Traffickers and Rehabilitating Thailand's Addicts

Lieut-Gen. Chavalit Yodmanee, who commands Thailand's assault on the heroin traffic domestically and for export, can claim some success in curbing domestic production of opium and heroin. In a recent interview, Chavalit said the challenge now is to coordinate efforts to go after the big-time international traffickers on the one hand, and rehabilitate Thailand's addicts on the other. In 1988, Chavalit's staff of 600 in the office of Narcotics Control Board doubled the previous year's record of heroin seizures, and has turned its focus to developing a drug rehabilitation programme. Under a new programme, those arrested for possession of heroin can enter a treatment centre rather than jail and so avoid a criminal record. Evidence that AIDS is spreading rapidly among heroin addicts has sparked Thailand's preventative approach, said Chavalit.

Thailand's neighbours to the south, Malaysia and Singapore, have taken the opposite tack. Both countries have a mandatory death sentence for possession of 15g or more of heroin, and there have been 81 executions for drug offences since 1975.

## Burma Is the Main Opium Producer

Burma is the main culprit for the near-panic over record opium production. Since mid-1988, when civil unrest led to a massive military crackdown in Rangoon and other urban centres, troops have been withdrawn from remote northern and eastern parts of the country, which have been Burma's traditional opium-growing areas. From 1984–87, according to a US General Accounting Office report released in September [1989], the Burmese army and police seized an average 1.5 tonnes of opium a year, and destroyed five heroin refineries as well as large tracts of opium fields.

Now, with little or no enforcement, and with foreign suspicion that some government officials are involved in the trade, opium warlords and ethnic insurgency groups are producing and refining with impunity, mainly in Shan and Kachin states, so that opium production after the 1989 harvest is estimated at more than 2,000 tonnes, compared with 1,200 tonnes the previous year. The figure is about double the estimated opium production in 1985. The number of heroin addicts in Burma, officially registered at 9,000, is reported to have risen dramatically over the past year [1989].

Also, because of the government's brutal crackdown on civil unrest in 1988, the US Government has cut off its US$14 million annual aid budget for the country, including an anti-narcotics effort which had cost Washington US$80 million from 1974–88. The assistance included US helicopters to police the anti-narcotics effort, and three Thrush aircraft to spray the controversial herbicide 24-D on opium fields.

## Farmers Return to Growing Opium

Without these controls, many opium farmers who had been forced into cultivating other crops have returned to growing opium, and many new farmers have turned to the lucrative cash crop. Further, ideal weather conditions have ensured rich harvests. And drug warlords, aware of the erosion of Burmese Government supervision, are refining more and more heroin over the border in Burma, rather than in northern Thailand, where Border Patrol Police have busted nine refineries this year.

While Burma remains the world's largest opium producer, with an annual yield that could meet the US market's demand of 60 tonnes 20 times over, Laos is also joining the big-time producer's club. Compared with Thailand's production of 25–35 tonnes of opium this year, Laos is estimated to have produced around 300 tonnes.

In northern Thailand, more hill tribes are being weaned away from opium production to other crops every year, under programmes launched by King Bhumibol Adulyadej and the UN. But narcotics officials in Bangkok say that while the effort in northern Thailand is laudable, booming opium production in neighbouring Burma and Laos renders it a drop in the ocean.

## Overworked Narcotics Police

Overworked narcotics police and military agents in Thailand, together with police agents from 14 countries allowed to keep a presence in Bangkok, are desperately trying—but with little success—to nab this bumper harvest on its way out of the country. US Deputy Secretary of State for Narcotics Affairs Melvyn Levitsky told a House panel in August, "an explosion of opium growing" in Asia has resulted in Southeast Asia supplying 42% of the heroin in the US—compared with about 15% in 1985.

The main reason why Thais and other Southeast Asians get hooked on heroin, as a "downer," rather than amphetamine stimulants favoured in Northeast Asia is that it is cheap and available. Many older-generation Thai-Chinese continue to smoke opium. In hill tribe areas, opium is used not only as a drug but as seasoning in cooking and as a pain-killer. Thailand banned opium use only in 1958.

With heroin becoming more and more plentiful, and perhaps even cheaper as the record Golden Triangle production seeks new markets, there will be few triumphs for Bangkok police and the ever-growing legion of international drug police.

# Heroin in the 1990s

*James A. Inciardi and Lana D. Harrison*

In the following selection James A. Inciardi and Lana D. Harrison describe the way heroin use spread beyond the inner city into mainstream culture in the 1990s. They say that heroin's growing popularity was due to its decreasing price and increasing purity. Because of this greater purity, heroin could be inhaled, thus eliminating the need for injections. Another popular way to use the drug was "chasing the dragon," the practice of heating and liquefying heroin on a piece of foil until vapors were emitted. The vapors were then "chased" into pipes and inhaled. The authors explain that several factors influenced how heroin was used, including age, race, gender, and years of use. They found that younger users and females were more likely to snort rather than inject the drug. They conclude that the number of heroin users was difficult to estimate due to a hidden population of users.

James A. Inciardi is a professor in the Department of Sociology and Criminal Justice at the University of Delaware and director of the university's Center for Drug and Alcohol Studies. Lana D. Harrison is also a professor in the Department of Sociology and Criminal Justice at the University of Delaware and is associate director of its Center for Drug and Alcohol Studies.

Heroin addiction has a long history in the United States and throughout the world. In Europe and the United States during the 1800s, opium and morphine were seen as miracle drugs and were used for a variety of ailments. This liberal use of opiates resulted in a vast number of addicts, many of whom were middle- and upper-class individuals who became addicted through medical use of the drugs. Complicating matters was the introduction of heroin in 1897 by Bayer Laboratories as a powerful cough suppressant. Since Bayer's heroin seemed to relieve the withdrawal symptoms associated with the use of other opiates, it was viewed by many as a cure for narcotic addiction, thus complicating matters even further. Since that time, of course, the addictive properties of heroin have been well publicized. Today [1998], the "typical" heroin addict is not viewed as someone who accidentally became dependent on the drug for medical reasons. Rather, the contemporary heroin "junkie"—a poor and often homeless resident of one of America's inner cities, who injects in back alleys or "shooting galleries"—is the image many people have of a heroin user.

## Heroin Has Moved into Mainstream

Recently, heroin use has to some extent moved beyond the inner city and into the mainstream culture. In the 1970s and 1980s, the deaths of such entertainers as Jimi Hendrix, Janis Joplin, and John Belushi brought attention to heroin use. During the [1990s], furthermore, heroin use has again become exceedingly visible in the popular culture. A number of popular rock bands have been linked to heroin use, through a member's overdose, arrest, or treatment/recovery. A small list includes Nirvana, Smashing Pumpkins, Red Hot Chili Peppers, and Depeche Mode. Hollywood has also played on heroin's popularity with recent movies such as *Pulp Fiction, Trainspotting,* and *Basketball Diaries.* And there is the fashion industry, promoting "heroin chic" images. Although Hollywood and the fashion and music industries are certainly not the causes of an emergent heroin epidemic, it is difficult not to see some parallels between what is happening in the worlds of entertainment and high fashion and the rise in heroin use in the mainstream culture.

## Heroin's Increased Marketability

A variety of factors have converged to increase the marketability of heroin. Heroin is cheaper now than it was in previous decades, thereby making it more affordable, especially for young people. In addition, the heroin on the market today is quite pure, more so than in decades past. In [the 1990s], heroin from Southeast Asia and Colombia has begun to dominate the U.S. market, especially in major metropolitan areas on the East Coast. It appears to be crowding out heroin from Southwest Asia and Mexico. Southeast Asian heroin is uniformly of very high purity. The implications are that it can readily be inhaled, thus obviating the necessity of injection, and it perhaps can even be smoked, although smoking heroin is still infrequent in the United States. Since the heroin available now is less expensive and still of good quality, routes of administration other than injection (intravenous heroin use is the most efficient means of administration), such as smoking, snorting/sniffing or "chasing" may be used.

## Routes of Administration

The ways in which users administer heroin vary throughout the world. The most popular routes of administration are smoking, inhaling or "chasing the dragon," sniffing/snorting, and injecting. Smoking heroin involves the dipping of cigarettes into heroin. Inhaling or "chasing" consists of heating heroin in a piece of foil until it becomes liquid. As the heroin runs over the surface of the foil, it emits a vapor, which is, in turn, "chased" into pipes and inhaled. Those who sniff/snort heroin do so in the same manner as those who snort cocaine—making lines or scooping the drug directly to the nose.

Just as there are variations in heroin use over time and location, there are variations in the routes used to administer the drug. Variables affecting one's choice of routing may include geography, purity, age of user, years of heroin use, and self-concept. According to [J.F.] French and [J.] Safford [in a 1989 article], the best predictors of whether a user will ingest heroin intranasally are age and years of use. The younger the users, the more likely they are to snort their heroin rather than inject it. Also, those who have used for 10 years or less are more likely to snort than those with heroin careers of longer duration.

Perhaps one reason why those with shorter heroin-using careers take their drugs nonintravenously is that they were first introduced to the drug through other routes of administration. In Chicago in 1993, researchers saw an increase in the number of young people being introduced to heroin through snorting, and associated increases in the number of opiate treatment admissions in which intranasal use was involved. In a study conducted in the United Kingdom, 95% of new users reported that their primary route of administration was not through injecting but through chasing. Also in the United Kingdom, researchers found that prior to 1978, most users were introduced to heroin through injecting the drug but that since that time, initiation has been through chasing. In fact, since 1985, chasing has become almost the exclusive route for first-time users.

Although age and years of use were found to be the best predictors of whether the user's primary route of administration was intranasal or smoking rather than injecting, other variables that had some predictive value were race (African Americans and Hispanics were more likely to be snorters), employment (snorters were more likely to be employed than intravenous users), and gender (females identified themselves as snorters more often than males). Gender was also found to be a factor in a study by Des Jarlais and colleagues (1994). In their examination of injection drug users in New York City, more than one third (37%) of those who reported intranasal ingestion of heroin as their primary route of administration were women.

## Prevalence of Heroin Use

The prevalence of heroin use has fluctuated over time, although the actual number of users is unknown. Two major

epidemics are recognized as occurring in the United States—
one that began after World War II and the other in the late
1960s, reaching its peak between 1971 and 1977. The United
States, furthermore, was not alone in experiencing a heroin
epidemic in the 1970s. Areas such as the United Kingdom,
Southeast and West Asia, and Western Europe, saw increases
in the use of heroin in the late 1970s. [G.] Anderson (1984) reports that during the mid-1980s, half of all young people (ages
between 14 and 25) who lived in the Merseyside region in England were regular heroin users.

Since the early 1960s, health and criminal justice organizations in the United States have been attempting to estimate the
number of heroin users for planning and policy purposes. In
1972, the Bureau of Narcotics and Dangerous Drugs estimated
that there were 559,224 users nationwide. One year later, the
Special Action Office for Drug Abuse Prevention put the number at 300,000, and in 1980, the National Institute on Drug
Abuse (NIDA) reported that the number was closer to 400,000.
In 1988, the Office of National Drug Control Policy (ONDCP)
estimated the number of casual users of heroin in the United
States to be 539,000 and the number of heavy users as
641,664. In 1991, these numbers fell to 381,492 and 586,132,
respectively. One can have only minimal confidence in any of
these numbers since we are dealing with hidden populations.
Most often, indicator data—such as criminal justice information on arrests, heroin seizures by law enforcement agencies,
or health indicator data such as treatment admissions and
hospital emergency room visits related to heroin use—are
used to provide some sense of overall changes in heroin use.

# CHAPTER THREE

# Opiates Today

# Methadone Is a Deadly Treatment for Heroin Addiction

*Theodore Dalrymple*

In this selection British physician Theodore Dalrymple accuses the British government of contributing to deaths of patients by encouraging doctors to prescribe methadone, a synthetic opiate used to treat heroin addiction. Methadone is extremely toxic in even small amounts and many people have died from methadone poisoning. Dalrymple also says that heroin addicts are selling large amounts of the prescribed methadone on the black market. Consequently, many who are dying of methadone poisoning are those who purchase the drug from heroin addicts. According to Dalrymple, Americans have followed the British example of dispensing methadone, also with disastrous results. For example, in Florida in 2001, the number of deaths from methadone poisoning surpassed those from heroin overdose. Dalrymple says that the only ethical way to dispense methadone is to require that heroin addicts ingest it at the time they receive it from the pharmacist. Methadone overdoses have been substantially lowered when this method is used. Theodore Dalrymple is a physician and psychiatrist who works in a British prison. He is the author of *Life at the Bottom: The Worldview That Makes the Underclass.*

The British government is bribing doctors to kill their patients and others. It wants (and will pay them) to prescribe methadone to heroin addicts, in the full knowledge that this will be done in so sloppy and irresponsible a fashion that many people will die as a result. He who wills the means, wills the ends.

The arguments for the prescription of methadone to heroin addicts are well known. Methadone is a synthetic opiate first developed in Nazi Germany during the war because of a shortage of opium supplies from the Far East. It was named dolphine in honour of a leader of the time (it is still sold under a similar brand name in the United States), and one of its first recipients was Hermann Goering, an addict whose criminality was not much reduced by its prescription.

## Methadone in Place of Heroin

Methadone is given mainly in liquid form, though it also exists as a pill and an injection, as a substitute for heroin. Its effects are long-lasting by comparison with those of heroin, so that it is taken only once a day. The rationale behind methadone treatment of drug addicts is that its prescription free of charge reduces the criminal activities of addicts, reduces their consumption of heroin and hence their risk-taking behaviour, and stabilises their day-to-day existence so that they are able to rejoin society, while eventually allowing them painlessly to reduce the dose little by little until they achieve total abstinence. Controlled trials have demonstrated the beneficial effects of methadone for groups of addicts.

Unfortunately, methadone is a very dangerous drug. Five millilitres—a teaspoonful—is enough to kill a baby, and 40ml is enough to kill an adult who is not habituated to opiates. The dangers are not merely theoretical, not even for the doctors who prescribe the stuff: from time to time one reads in the medical press of doctors who have been struck off the medical register for negligently believing the lies their patients tell them about the amount of methadone they take, amounts that promptly kill their patients.

## Deaths from Methadone

Deaths from methadone are by no means negligible in number. In Florida in 2001, deaths from methadone poisoning surpassed those from heroin poisoning for the first time, by 133 to 121. Meanwhile, back in Blighty [Great Britain], to demonstrate that we are also in the vanguard of modernity, deaths from methadone have been rising steadily. Between 1993 and 2000, there were 4,058 deaths from the direct effects of heroin; in the same period, there were 2,500 deaths from methadone. Since far fewer than a third of addicts receive methadone, it is at least as likely, to put it no stronger, that methadone kills rather than saves.

A large percentage of those who die of methadone poisoning are not those who are prescribed it, but purchasers of methadone from those who receive it free and use the proceeds to buy heroin (and sometimes children of addicts who are attracted to the bright green sweet liquid). Diversion of methadone on to the black market is so widespread that the price is low: currently about 1 [pound sterling] for 10ml. Addicts are able to sell their methadone because they are prescribed bottles of it at a time.

The diversion of this dangerous substance on to the black market—where it kills—hardly gives our distinguished government pause, or slows the self-propelled juggernaut of the drug addiction treatment industry. And there could be no clearer illustration of how those who work in the field of drug addiction have become a self-serving bureaucracy than the response of an Australian in the field to the fact that in New South Wales 46 per cent of those who die of methadone poisoning have never been prescribed it: "The large proportion of deaths involving diverted methadone may suggest a high unmet demand for methadone and/or a need to make methadone maintenance treatment attractive to a greater diversity of dependent heroin users." As a physician friend of mine at the hospital in which I work remarked (where, incidentally, we have treated 51 methadone overdoses in the past 18 months, many requiring intensive care), this is a little like concluding from the existence of rape that there is an unmet demand for sex.

As it happens, it is not inevitable that the prescription of methadone must be accompanied by so many deaths. In Glasgow, for instance, the number of people prescribed methadone increased from 140 in 1992 to 2,800 in 1998. But the number of deaths from methadone in the city increased from three to seven, that is to say they declined proportionately by 86 per cent.

## An Ethical Way to Administer Methadone

The reason for this was obvious: Glasgow instituted a policy according to which those prescribed methadone had to take it in front of the dispensing pharmacist each day, and were not given a supply that they could turn into cash. Ninety per cent of methadone prescriptions were dispensed in this fashion: if it had been 100 per cent, the deaths would have been even fewer. Clearly, this method of prescription must have been acceptable to addicts, since so many of them agreed to it.

These figures suggest, indeed, that it is the only ethically acceptable method of prescription: all other methods are tantamount to murder, or at least culpable homicide. Yet the latter methods will remain predominant for the foreseeable future, as most places have not instituted the Glaswegian approach. The death of a drug addict or one of those people inclined to buy methadone on the black market probably saves the British taxpayer a considerable sum of money in the long run, or even the short run, but this is surely taking the desirable principle of economising where possible a little far. Incidentally, the rise in deaths from methadone in America is probably attributable to the adoption of British methods. For once, the Americans are copying us, with predictably disastrous results.

## Methadone and Criminality

There is another, wider objection to methadone maintenance treatment, however—or indeed any form of treatment of drug addicts. It is astonishing to me that the authors of trials which demonstrate a reduction of criminality among addicts when prescribed methadone conclude that the prescription of methadone will reduce the total amount of allegedly drug-fuelled crime in society.

Not only is the relationship between criminality and drug-taking much more complex than the "feed-my-habit" conception usually peddled (the decision to take heroin is also a conscious way of opting for the criminal life, because no one any longer is ignorant of the consequences of taking the drug), but it does not follow that, if criminality is reduced among treated addicts, criminality as a whole decreases.

If you were a drug dealer with a customer who told you that, thanks to methadone (or any other treatment), you no longer required his wares, would you simply accept the contraction of your market, or would you act as any salesman would act when one customer fails to buy? Thus, it is possible that, with treatment, we end up with a methadone addict and a heroin addict, whereas before we had only a heroin addict.

## Treatment Has Spread Heroin Addiction

Does this fit what has actually happened in Britain better than, say, the tuberculosis model of methadone treatment? When a patient has infectious TB, treating him is not only therapeutic for him but preventive for the public: it interrupts the transmission of the disease. But the apparatus of treatment for drug addiction is more likely to spread the problem—I won't call it a disease—than to cure or prevent it. The number of people receiving methadone in this country has reached 30,000, but heroin continues to cut a swathe through the lower reaches of society. Opium (loosely construed) has become the opium of the masses.

Neither methadone nor any other medicalised "treatment" will solve the social problem of heroin addiction. On the contrary, it will increase it.

True, a doctor has to do his best for the individual patient who consults him: he treats an individual's problems, not those of society and therefore can quite ethically, on the basis of published research, come to the conclusion that methadone is the best available solution to his patient's current problem—provided that the methadone is swallowed in front of a pharmacist. It is not his concern if, by prescribing the wretched stuff, he is encouraging the spread of heroin yet further.

## No Technical Solution for Heroin Addiction

Speaking to hundreds of addicts, as I do, it is evident that, considered as a whole, the problem is a deep social, psychological, cultural, moral, educational and spiritual one. There is no technical fix for it, not now and not in the future. Biomedical research, however fascinating it may be from the point of view of disinterested intellectual curiosity, will not provide a solution.

The poor abandoned addicts whom I see every day of my life have never had a father, have never eaten a meal at a table with other people, have nothing in their minds but pop music and football. They are the new wretched of the earth, and there is no medicine for their wretchedness.

# Methadone Is an Effective Treatment for Heroin Addiction

*Alex Wodak*

The following selection is taken from a study in which Alex Wodak says that treatment with methadone is the most effective, safe, and cost-effective treatment for heroin addiction. Wodak says methadone treatment offers major health benefits to individuals and communities, including a reduction in HIV infections. He believes that methadone treatment has been limited because of underfunding and hostile public attitudes toward heroin users. Governments in many countries spend considerably more on drug law enforcement than on drug treatment. Consequently, Wodak says, methadone programs are too short and do not provide the high doses necessary to be effective.

Alex Wodak is a physician and the director of the Alcohol and Drug Service at St. Vincent's Hospital in Sydney, Australia. Wodak is also president of the Australian Drug Law Reform Foundation and president of the International Harm Reduction Association.

Methadone treatment is a compromise. Most drug users enrolled in methadone treatment have come to a point in their lives where they believe they cannot continue to consume street heroin, although many would still prefer heroin if a free choice were available. Many in our community [Australia] now recognize that drug users, their families, and their communities are far better off if the majority of drug users are enrolled in treatment, while also acknowledging that no other treatment is as successful as methadone. But many community members would far prefer treatment to never involve the use of a mood-altering and addictive drug like methadone. The battles waged over methadone are largely symbolic conflicts reflecting this uneasy peace. The entrenched belief in many communities that supply-control measures [eradicating drug supplies to control drug use] are effective, against vast and compelling evidence, leads inexorably to the powerful discrimination and poor health outcomes experienced by drug users. This stigma in turn affects those few clinicians prepared to accept a professional responsibility to improve the health and social functioning of drug users. Many of the most egregious deficiencies of methadone treatment are the inevitable consequences of community fear and loathing for people who choose to use heroin.

## Lack of Resources

It is important that treatment providers and consumers alike recognize the source of most of the problems that are so common and so similar in methadone treatment systems all over the world. Extreme scarcity of resources for methadone treatment is virtually universal and reflects the deep uneasiness of communities about drug use and people who use drugs. This resource scarcity causes severe distortions to the treatment system that providers and consumers both resent. All over the world demand for methadone treatment outstrips supply. But surely that cannot be considered the fault of methadone treatment? All over the world methadone is virtually the only pharmacotherapeutic treatment option available for people with heroin dependence. If treatment providers had their way, methadone would be readily available and would be just one of several pharmacotherapeutic options for people with heroin dependence. In any other potentially life-threatening condition with major public health impact, effective treatment is made readily available and is not artificially constrained to one agent. As of now [2002], heroin users can have whatever pharmacotherapeutic option they want, provided it is methadone.

The common negative perceptions of methadone treatment matter a great deal because this intervention provides such major health, social, and economic benefit to drug users, their families, and the communities they live in. Few other treatments in medicine have been subjected to so much research scrutiny and few other treatments are so well supported by evidence of benefit. The health benefits are major and exist at both individual and population levels. For example, over 30 studies have concluded that methadone treatment reduces HIV infection. In most countries, data and evidence play only a minor role, whereas the widespread contempt for drug users has a major influence in policy decisions made about the size and quality of the methadone treatment system. Consequently, many clinicians working in this area spend a considerable part of their time advocating for a treatment that they know provides immense benefits, notwithstanding its undeniable faults.

## Methadone Treatment Attracts Heroin Users

It is salutary to remember that methadone must always be compared with the few other realistic options. Few severely dependent heroin users are better off managing with adulterated street heroin of unknown concentration than in methadone treatment. Even poor-quality methadone treatment is a far more humane and beneficial option for drug users than incarceration. In all countries, methadone treatment attracts and retains many more heroin users than any other treatment modality. The findings of this study are no exception. More than two-thirds (70%) of the drug users taking part in interviews had ever wanted to be in a drug treatment program, and three-quarters (75%) had experienced drug treatment. Almost half (49%) had been in (presumably lengthy episodes of) methadone treatment, which was a greater proportion than any other option apart from detoxification. In a recent study, a substantial proportion of heroin-dependent individuals given a choice between heroin or methadone prescription preferred the latter.

From the perspective of non-drug-using members of the community, methadone treatment is also a considerably better option for drug users than street heroin, other forms of drug-user treatment (where heroin users usually only remain for a few weeks), or incarceration. This is true both in terms of outcomes as well as cost effectiveness. The most costly option for non-drug users is to have heroin users neither in drug-user treatment nor incarcerated.

## Methadone Treatment Is Too Short

The fact that many heroin users often try methadone treatment multiple times but leave treatment prematurely reflects in part the relapsing–remitting nature of drug use. The more hostile the environment to drug use and drug users, the more we can expect methadone treatment to fail to reflect research findings. In the United States, most methadone treatment fails to implement research findings and most research findings never get implemented. Higher methadone dose and longer duration of treatment have been shown consistently to powerfully predict methadone treatment success, yet study after study in North America reports clinical trials with doses and durations of treatment known to be suboptimal. The failure to implement research findings, a consequence of the hostile drug-policy environment, leads directly to poor-quality programs, inadequate retention, unsatisfactory outcomes for all stakeholders, and unethical research. In most parts of the world today, the retention rates for methadone treatment quoted in this paper would be regarded as totally unacceptable. The fact that they are tolerated in Canada reflects the more hostile environment that methadone treatment has to contend with in that country than in many other parts of the world.

## Problems for Those in Treatment

Some of the complaints about methadone by treatment consumers also reflect community contempt of drug use that has been internalized by heroin injectors. In a world that discriminates so egregiously against people with minority sexual preferences, many homosexuals internalize homophobia. Is it surprising that many drug users become deeply ambivalent about their drug use and, like many members of the community, confuse the proposed solution with the original problem?

A number of the criticisms of methadone programs by treatment consumers refer to problems that are very common and that also often upset staff. For example, many of the absurdities involving urine testing are concessions treatment providers are often forced to make to funding bodies in order to maintain the existence of a treatment they know to be very valuable to treatment consumers and the community alike.

Another source of misunderstanding of the nature of methadone programs is the characteristics of many patients in methadone treatment. Severe disadvantage is common, including serious mental health problems, limited education, long-term unemployment, debt, poverty, residential instability, and squalor. It would be foolhardy to ignore these major factors when we consider how well or badly these programs manage communication between patients and staff. These are not excuses to justify the provision of inferior-quality treatment but they do make it easy to understand why programs are often misunderstood. Some common patient concerns about methadone are urban myths whose survival depends on the combination of an environment hostile to mood-altering drugs and internalized *"addictophobia."* For example, there is no evidence that methadone damages the immune system or the liver. Comparisons between the difficulties experienced by individuals withdrawing from heroin or methadone show surprisingly little difference, yet the urban myth survives.

# Treating Opiate Addiction as a Central Nervous System Disorder

*Andre Waismann*

In this selection Andre Waismann argues that the scientific community should view opiate dependency as a medical illness rather than as a psychosocial disorder. Waismann believes that opiate dependency is a central nervous system disorder that requires medical assessment and treatment. He explains that methadone is an ineffective treatment for opiate addiction because it masks the problem and replaces one dependency with another. Instead, he has developed a process he calls neuroregulation, in which patients are treated with medications and sedated so that they can go through withdrawal while unconscious. Patients are then prescribed Naltrexone, a nonaddictive medication that reduces opiate cravings in the brain. Waismann emphasizes that physicians should treat their opiate-dependent patients nonjudgmentally and with respect. Andre Waismann is a surgeon and trauma specialist in Beverly Hills, California, and is the founder of the Waismann Institute for Treatment of Opiate Dependency.

Substance abuse unquestionably is a major health concern in the U.S. and the world, with annual treatment costs in the billions of dollars. The social impact in relation to crime, family life, and lost productivity is immeasurable. Diseases such as hepatitis C and AIDS have become common in many communities. Heroin, one of many opiate drugs, is the key player in this rapidly growing dilemma. Opiate-dependent babies have become an everyday reality in many cities, and heroin use among eighth-, 10th-, and 12th-graders has significantly increased over the last decade [of the twentieth century]. Based on the most recently published statistics by the National Institute on Drug Abuse, 600,000 people in the U.S. are addicted to heroin.

Remedies in the past have included addictive opiate replacements and long-term isolation from society in centers outside general hospitals. Rehabilitation centers were developed to offer opiate dependents an array of alternatives, all of which involved suffering through long and tormenting withdrawal symptoms. Detoxification procedures often require lengthy and costly inpatient hospitalization, with dropout rates of 30 to 50% for inpatient and 70% for outpatient clinics. Despite these statistics, governmental institutions continue to support centers for treatment of opiate-dependent patients outside general hospitals and outside the realm of mainstream medicine.

## Methadone Is Not the Answer

Methadone has become the treatment of choice and is widely endorsed by the scientific community as an effective remedy for heroin addiction. In fact, methadone masks the problem and simply replaces one dependency with another. Abstinence achieved by regular detoxification, psychotherapy, and methadone maintenance is not the solution.

Throughout the years, patients' demands have been in direct opposition to the options for available treatment. Most patients desired freedom from the dependency, and tried abstinence without medical assistance. As a consequence, "cold turkey" became recognized as a valid treatment. When a no-treatment

treatment became a workable idea, many experts were willing to apply therapeutic values to vomiting, pain, diarrhea, and other symptoms of withdrawal. Statements such as "no pain, no gain" became part of many physicians' vocabularies. The scientific community continues to ignore the need to challenge the existing perceptions of opiate dependency and treatment.

## Scientific Failure to Treat Opiate Addiction

Biotechnology has reached achievements in the clinical field of medicine unimaginable for a physician from the 1950s or 1960s. Yet, little has changed on the clinical level for an opiate-dependent patient. It is almost impossible to identify developments and improvements in the level of care, even in the most prestigious centers in the world, despite the incredible budgets for research invested in this subject. Opiate dependency seems to be perceived as an incurable condition. The scientific community has failed to challenge this concept, as well as the stereotypical view that dependent individuals have addictive or weak personalities.

For more than 30 years, opioid receptor management, through the use of agonists and antagonists, has become a standard technique used by anesthesiologists and other medical practitioners. However, all of the knowledge and techniques developed during those years in the medical field were not applied to the treatment of opiate dependency. The reason? Opiate dependency was not initially classified as a medical illness, but, rather, as a psychosocial condition. The scientific community has failed to challenge this classification.

Treatment today sees most opiate-dependent people being treated by ex-opiate-dependent individuals, social workers, psychologists, and psychiatrists. The treatment options include rehabilitation and/or detoxification centers, methadone clinics, hotel rooms, religious entities, and a few other alternatives. Despite the range of treatments available, patients are not afforded the common option offered to any other patient suffering from an illness—to go to a hospital and have the illness assessed in a professional environment with respect and dignity.

## Neuroregulation as Treatment

Opiate dependency is a central nervous system disorder. The primary stage of the illness is withdrawal, and opiate craving is one of the secondary by-products. Therefore, detoxification procedures combined with any other counseling therapy cannot effectively access the root of the illness. Instead, neuroregulation should be the method of treatment, and this withdrawal management should be combined with craving relief. Without immediate and effective treatment, secondary social effects result. Social dysfunction and the need for social rehabilitation are often linked to the length of time and the severity of the illness endured by the dependent individual.

A physician's duty is to provide the patient at the onset of illness with an effective, safe, and humane treatment to reverse the condition. I find that psychosocial side effects can be prevented. At the first signs of the illness, when the patient has realized that he or she is hooked and needs to cope with the situation, going to a methadone clinic or enduring a long and painful stay at a detoxification center is often not considered. The patient sees cold turkey as the only option. Most patients will try and try again, with no success. Throughout the process, the patient may resort to lying, hiding, and hunting for self-healing. It becomes an everyday reality.

Each time a patient tries to overcome dependency and fails, he or she becomes discouraged, often to the extent that dependency is more appealing than another attempt. This sequence of events cause the psychosocial side effects. Based on my professional experience, the psychosocial aspects of opiate dependency are not the cause of the illness, but, rather, the secondary effects of the untreated dependency.

As with so many aspects of life, rules and regulations should follow the advancement of technology. The legal systems should adapt to a new paradigm where opiate craving is recognized as a biological condition. On this basis, punishment or imprisonment are not adequate methods to prevent relapse. Instead, effective medical assessment and treatment should be utilized to achieve better outcomes.

If one were to measure, on a scale, the level of opiate cravings a patient has one month prior to the first withdrawal syndrome, it would be found to be very low. Immediately after the first withdrawal, the craving scale would rise to higher levels. Even if the patient were successfully to overcome the withdrawal, the cravings would be higher than they were prior to dependency. Additionally, the craving scale rises in direct proportion to the length of time of the dependency. In other words, the longer the patient remains dependent, the higher the craving scale would be, even after a successful withdrawal. For years, as with most aspects of opiate dependency, craving has been linked to the many psychosocial aspects associated with dependency, with very few attempts to identify the neurological roots on the opioid receptor level.

In advanced medicine, doctors should recognize that any bodily dysfunction generates physical and psychological distress. On the clinical level, they cannot disregard either and, if possible, should intervene on both levels at once, taking into consideration the effects of one on the other. With the tools available today, it is necessary to take the focus off the methods that aren't working and invest in alternatives that do.

## Treatment with Medication

In the [late 1990s], modern biotechnology has allowed physicians increasingly to understand the process of receptors within the brain that work to regulate opiates. Recognizing this opportunity, I developed a process called neuroregulation, which focuses on treating opiate dependency at the receptor level. This approach blocks the opiate receptors in the brain to precipitate the withdrawal syndrome, while, at the same time, controlling it. This is achieved through the use of medications, including anesthetic agents that allow withdrawal to occur throughout the procedure while the patient is unconscious. Patients undergo a comprehensive psychological and medical examination prior to the commencement of the treatment conducted in a hospital intensive care unit. A patient can expect to be hospitalized for 24 to 36 hours, including the four-hour period allotted for the sedation process. Upon discharge, patients are prescribed a regimen of Naltrexone, a nonaddictive and non-mood-altering medication that ensures the patient will abstain from craving opiates.

Most patients will take a regular dose of Naltrexone for a year following the procedure. Naltrexone is FDA-approved, as are all the medications used in the procedure, and has been utilized for approximately 30 years in the medical field. No serious side effects have been associated with it. If properly prescribed, Naltrexone will effectively prevent and have a reversal effect on craving. The main reason for the maintenance dose is to keep the patient's opiate receptors in the brain blocked against the impact of opiates in order to eliminate the cravings or the psychological need for them. Thereafter, the patient is able to resume a healthy and productive life.

## Helping with Chronic Pain Management

In addition, this approach has opened the doors of pain-management treatment to patients who endure pain despite increased medication dosages [of opiates]. With increased dosages, patients can develop opiate dependency, leading to drug-tolerance levels so high no pain relief can be achieved. Remove the dependency, and patients can return to a more appropriate and effective, opiate-free, pain-management treatment program. Throughout the years, such treatments have effectively reversed opiate dependency in patients suffering from chronic pain caused by car accidents, war injuries, or illness and have assisted in improving their quality of life.

Patients with diabetes, chronic heart conditions, and AIDS, among other illnesses, are now able to receive safe treatment. Until recently, such individuals often were left to live with their dependency, due to the high risk involved in treating patients with these conditions or their inability to endure the pain associated with withdrawal symptoms. Neuroregulation offers these patients a safe and humane alternative to their suffering and a treatment enabling them to get beyond addiction.

In 1997, I reversed opiate dependency in a six-year-old child who was hooked on morphine for five years following surgery and a pain-management program that used opiates. It is time to shift the treatment of "heroin babies" and replace the long, painful, and sometimes damaging current approaches with a timely, humane, and effective technique.

## The Benefits of Neuroregulation

Neuroregulation reduces the risks of anesthesia-related complications and has proven to ensure positive outcomes. Future practices must focus on giving patients precise and scientific information regarding opiate dependency. The goal is to offer an effective way of overcoming withdrawal and managing cravings with medicinal tools. The idea is to free patients from misguided theories and provide them with the knowledge and treatment they deserve.

The neuroregulation approach has changed the direction of opiate dependency treatment and brings about a new understanding of what was once perceived as addiction and is now recognized as neuroadaptation. The breakthroughs in changing the direction of treating opiate dependency assist in continually elevating the standard of care and research work necessary in meeting these ideologies in healing. Opiate addiction is a disorder of the central nervous system that can be reversed with appropriate medical treatment.

The challenge remains to release patients from all the misguided theories they were made to believe for so long, providing them with the knowledge and treatment they deserve and the freedom of choice they are entitled to. Regardless of patients' decisions and their overall outcome, the physician's role is not to confront and judge them, but to treat them with all of the knowledge and technology available to assess their needs. This is part of a very old oath undertaken by the scientific community that has unfortunately been forgotten by many.

# Physicians Prescribe Heroin in the United Kingdom

*Gerry V. Stimson and Nicky Metrebian*

The United Kingdom is one of the few countries where physicians are allowed to prescribe heroin as a treatment for those addicted to opiates. In this selection taken from a British report on prescription heroin, Gerry V. Stimson and Nicky Metrebian outline the arguments for and against using heroin to treat people who are dependent on the drug. The authors explain the history of the practice in the United Kingdom, stating that whereas the United States criminalized heroin abuse early in the twentieth century, the United Kingdom treated it as a medical problem. British physicians were advised to prescribe heroin or morphine to addicts if it would allow them to lead "normal and useful lives." In the 1970s, however, doctors turned away from prescribing heroin and instead tried to persuade patients to use methadone as a substitute drug. In the 1990s the government once again enacted a policy to encourage the prescription of heroin in order to reduce some of the crime associated with illegal drug sales.

Gerry V. Stimson is head of the Department of Social Science and Medicine and director of the Centre for Research on Drugs and Health Behaviour at the Imperial College of Medicine in London. Nicky Metrebian is a research fellow at the Department of Social Science and Medicine at the Imperial College in London.

Gerry V. Stimson and Nicky Metrebian, "Prescribing Heroin: What Is the Evidence?" *Findings Report # 943*, Drug and Alcohol Series, September 2003, pp. 1–8. Copyright © 2003 by the Joseph Rowntree Foundation. Reproduced by permission.

The UK is exceptional internationally because heroin is included in the range of legally sanctioned treatments for opiate dependence. In practice, this treatment option is rarely utilised: only about 448 heroin users receive heroin on prescription. Some people would like to see heroin prescribed to more people who are dependent on it. But an increase in prescribing heroin may have benefits as well as risks. Coming to a judgement on the merits of prescribing heroin for the treatment of opiate dependence requires looking at scant research evidence to determine whether heroin prescribing is likely to have an advantage over other treatments for dependence.

## Those in Favour

Those in favour of prescribing heroin for the treatment of opiate dependence often point to the following in support of their case:

- Current treatments—mainly methadone substitution—are insufficiently attractive or effective for some heroin addicts. Prescribing heroin users their drug of choice might attract more people into treatment and retain them in treatment for longer. More heroin users would get help and there would be fewer untreated heroin users in the community.
- It may help some people to stop or reduce their illicit heroin use; this would undercut the black market in illicit heroin; and ensure that heroin users can use a drug of known quality and strength.
- It may help people avoid health problems (such as overdose) and unsafe injecting practices that can lead to transmission of HIV and hepatitis B and C (HBV, HCV).
- It may lead to less acquisitive crime to support a drug habit and to improved social functioning (work, housing and family life).
- It is a first step that may facilitate a gradual change away from heroin use to methadone, and from injecting to oral use.

- Individual heroin users would benefit—and so would society—by having less drug-related crime, lower criminal justice and prison costs, fewer or less visible drug markets, lower aggregate healthcare costs, and lower social welfare costs.

## Those Against

Those who do not favour the medical prescription of heroin, or who are more cautious, often point to the following:

- It might maintain the condition of dependence by removing the motivation to stop using or injecting drugs. It might prolong the time a heroin user is drug dependent and injecting.
- An accumulating population of patients receiving a prescription for heroin prevents others from getting treatment.
- Individuals might suffer adverse health consequences as a result of continued heroin injecting (even though the drug is prescribed), including risk of overdose, infections, abscesses and blood-borne viruses, e.g. HIV and HCV.
- Society would have more heroin users and an increasing burden of ill-health.
- Pharmaceutical heroin is more expensive than methadone. Society has finite resources so needs to allocate them equitably.
- Heroin users presenting for treatment would come to expect heroin and might not accept alternatives such as oral methadone.
- There would be potential for diversion of prescribed heroin onto the illicit market, with the danger that new heroin users would be created.
- It is better to use treatments of known effectiveness such as methadone.

Heroin is prescribed in the treatment of opiate dependence in only a few countries.

In the UK, heroin has been prescribed to treat opiate dependence since the 1920s. It was originally adopted to help drug addicts lead normal lives without needing to purchase illegal drugs. More recently, the UK government has proposed the limited expansion of heroin prescribing because of the potential impact of such a strategy on reducing crime as well as improving the health of heroin users.

Scientific trials of heroin treatment have been completed in Switzerland and the Netherlands. Switzerland has now authorised the prescription of heroin for opiate dependence. Since 1998, heroin can be prescribed in the Netherlands for research purposes.

Scientific trials on the efficacy of heroin prescribing are planned or are taking place in Germany, France, Belgium, Spain and Canada [as of 2002]. In 1992, Australia undertook research studies on the feasibility of prescribing heroin but the proposed trial did not take place, reputedly because of outside pressure on the Australian government.

## Who Wants to Increase Heroin Prescribing?

The *Updated Drug Strategy* for the UK states that the medical prescription of heroin will be available for all those who have a clinical need. This policy is part of the government's aim to break the cycle of drug misuse and crime by providing effective treatment and rehabilitation. In its review of the government's drug policy, the Home Affairs Committee also recommended that a pilot programme of prescribing heroin be conducted, targeted in the first instance at chronic heroin users who are prolific offenders. It also made recommendations for a trial to look at the prescription of heroin to addicts with a long history of addiction who have not yet gained access to treatment or who are not currently in treatment. It is interesting to note that, in the UK, prescribing heroin is seen—at least by government—more as a way of reducing drug-related crime than as a public health strategy to reduce the risk of HIV infection or mortality due to overdose.

There is also support for heroin prescribing from the Liberal Democratic party. Its Home Affairs spokesperson Simon Hughes said: 'Heroin should be available on prescription because obtaining it through safe outlets is much safer than forcing addicts back into the hands of dealers'. The Association of Chief Police Officers asserted that:

> . . . there is a compelling case to explore further the merits of prescribing drugs of addiction to patients with entrenched dependency problems who have not responded to other forms of therapy. . . . This should include the wider use of heroin within a menu of treatments.

Chief Superintenent John Issac of Devon and Cornwall Police told BBC's *Newsnight*:

> There will always be a debate among the medical profession about the ethics of prescribing heroin. But from a police officer's point of view, I have to say that if it reduces crime, reduces the number of victims, that has to be a very serious consideration. And I would support it.

## History of Prescribing Heroin

Worldwide, drug treatments have been influenced by international agreements to control drugs, and by changing ideas about the nature of the 'heroin problem' and how to solve it. As we have already seen, some see prescribing heroin as a way to reduce the problem of drug-related crime and others emphasise the advantages of heroin prescribing as a way of reducing public health problems (e.g. overdoses, infectious diseases).

The international control of heroin began in 1909 in Shanghai at a special commission convened by the USA. A convention signed in The Hague in 1912 limited the manufacture, distribution and use of heroin to medical use. This was as a result of the growing opium trade (heroin is an opiate derived from opium), which had come under increased criticism because of the increasing numbers of individuals addicted to heroin. As a result, in the USA, the 1914 Harrison Narcotic Act restricted the use of opiates to legitimate medical purposes and, by 1919, doctors could be prosecuted for prescribing opiates to addicts. In the UK, the Dangerous Drugs Act of 1920 restricted the supply of morphine and heroin to registered medical practitioners for the purpose of medical treatment. In 1956, with the Narcotic Drug Control Act, the medical use of heroin was completely withdrawn in the USA and many other countries (although hospitals were allowed to continue using existing stocks of heroin).

Many countries believe (erroneously) that the international drug conventions prohibit the use of heroin in medical treatment. Furthermore, the International Narcotics Control Board

## THE HISTORY OF DRUGS

# The 1926 Recommendations

Circumstances in which morphine or heroin may legitimately be administered to addicts:

There are two groups of persons suffering from addiction to whom the administration of morphine or heroin may be regarded as legitimate medical treatment, namely:

a. Those who are undergoing treatment for cure of addiction by the gradual reduction method;

b. Persons for whom, after every effort has been made for the cure of addiction, the drug cannot be completely withdrawn, either because:

i. complete withdrawal produces serious symptoms which cannot be satisfactorily treated under the ordinary conditions of private practice, or where:

ii. a patient, who while capable of leading a useful and fairly normal life so long as he takes a certain nonprogressive quantity, usually small, of the drug of addiction, ceases to be able to do so when the regular allowance is withdrawn.

Departmental Committee on Morphine and Heroin Addiction, 1926.

(INCB) has exerted great pressure on countries to cease prescribing heroin for any medical purpose. Nevertheless, a few countries, including the UK, Belgium, the Netherlands, Iceland, Malta, Canada and Switzerland, continue to use heroin (diamorphine) for general medical purposes, mostly in hospital settings (usually for severe pain relief). Until recently, however, Britain was the only country that allowed doctors to prescribe heroin for the treatment of drug dependence.

## Heroin Prescribing in the UK

Prescribing heroin and other opiate drugs has been part of the British response to opiate dependence since the 1920s. While the USA chose to criminalise heroin dependency, Britain chose to medicalise the problem. In the UK, the reasons for prescribing heroin have changed over the last 100 years reflecting different historical contexts and changing perceptions of 'the problem'.

## 1920s–1960s: Helping Addicts Lead Normal Lives

In the early 1920s, the extent of the opiate problem in the UK was very small, with few individuals dependent on morphine and even fewer on heroin. In 1926, the Rolleston Committee was convened to consider and advise as to the circumstances, if any, in which the prescription of heroin or morphine to addicts was medically advised. This report recommended that medical practitioners could prescribe heroin or morphine to addicts if it would enable patients to lead useful lives. Thus, from the late 1920s, it was considered *bona fide* medical practice to maintain addicts on their drug of addiction if other treatments had failed and if they were able to live 'normal and useful lives' when given a regular, stable dose but were unable to do so when the supply of the drug was withdrawn. Until 1968, any doctor could prescribe heroin or other opiate drugs in the treatment of opiate dependence. The majority of doctors who prescribed heroin were general practitioners.

This approach worked reasonably well with the addict population of the time, most of who were in the medical and nursing professions and who became addicted because they had access to opiates; others were individuals who had become addicted in the course of medical treatment (known as therapeutic or iatrogenic addicts).

## Mid-1960s: Prescribing to Contain the Black Market

In 1961, the Brain Committee was established (Interdepartmental Committee on Drug Addiction) to consider whether the prescribing policy (based on Rolleston) should be revised and whether there was a medical need to provide special treatment outside the resources already available. It concluded that the drug problem was still small. The Committee saw no reason for any changes in existing practice or procedures.

However, at the beginning of the 1960s, there was a sharp increase in the numbers of heroin users. These were 'hedonistic' heroin users—individuals using heroin initially 'recreationally' and for pleasure, and associated with a 'deviant' or 'underground' culture. The doctors who prescribed heroin thought they were helping to contain an illicit market in heroin. They little realised that some of the heroin that they were prescribing was being sold and therefore they, by prescribing heroin, were helping the black market to expand. Some heroin users received very large prescriptions for heroin and were selling some of it.

Concerns about the increase in numbers of known heroin users led to the establishment of the Second Brain Committee. The Committee (Interdepartmental Committee on Drug Addiction, 1965) blamed the increase in heroin use on the doctors who were overly generous in their prescribing, stating that 'the majority source of supply has been the activity of a very few doctors who have prescribed excessively for addicts'. At the time of report, several doctors were prescribing heroin and cocaine in very large quantities. The Brain Committee recommended that restrictions should apply to the prescribing of heroin and that 'treatment centres be set up, mainly in London and might form part of a psychiatric hospital or the psychiatric wing of a general hospital'. In effect, the report recommended that, to control the problem, the right to prescribe heroin for the treatment of addiction should be restricted to psychiatrists working at special drug clinics. This report informed new legislation.

## The Dangerous Drug Act

In 1967, the Dangerous Drug Act restricted the prescribing of heroin and cocaine in the treatment of addiction to doctors holding licences from the Home Office. Prescribing heroin in the treatment of other medical conditions was unaffected. In 1968, new specialist drug dependency units (DDUs) were established by the Ministry of Health—mainly in London. The licensed doctors were mostly NHS psychiatrists in charge of the DDUs—thus effectively excluding general practitioners from prescribing heroin for the treatment of opiate dependence.

One reason for prescribing heroin—given by the Ministry of Health at that time and some of the doctors in the clinics—was to contain the spread of the 'epidemic'. Doctors tried to prescribe just enough to tempt people into treatment, but not too much because this might feed the illicit drug market. Some described this as 'competitive prescribing'—doctors competing against the illicit drug market by maintaining heroin users on just the right dose. Too much and they might sell it, too little and they might turn to the illicit drug market.

## 1970s: The Shift from Heroin to Methadone

After 1970, prescribing heroin went out of favour and doctors at the clinics started to persuade patients to change to methadone as a substitute drug.

This shift was influenced by a number of reasons. These included concerns over the potential threat of the diversion to the black market of prescribed heroin, growing optimism about the positive therapeutic effects of methadone and its advantages over heroin, and concerns with the safety of continued injecting of heroin. Many doctors considered that prescribing heroin was 'feeding a habit' while prescribing methadone was a 'medical treatment'. Steadily accumulating clinic caseloads of patients maintained long term on heroin, and drug workers' disenchantment with maintaining heroin users on heroin, also contributed to the shift of opinion. Moreover, doctors became more interested in abstinence than maintenance as a treatment goal.

There was little conclusive research evidence to support this change away from prescribing heroin and no formal change of drug policy. Rather, it was as a result of doctors' decisions and peer pressure within the medical profession. Contributing to the support for this change in treatment were the results of a randomised controlled trial conducted by Richard Hartnoll and Martin Mitcheson comparing heroin maintenance with oral methadone maintenance. The results of the trial were inconclusive and the authors' conclusions cautious.

Hartnoll and Mitcheson found that those receiving a prescription for heroin tended to stay in treatment but continued to inject and use illicit drugs, although in smaller amounts than before entering treatment. Those receiving oral methadone went to one extreme or another: either they stopped using illicit drugs completely or they continued to be heavily involved in drugs and dropped out of treatment.

The results identified advantages and disadvantages of both treatments. But the results were interpreted by many to show that oral methadone was preferable, and that heroin encouraged continued drug use and led to steadily accumulating clinic populations. The research provided a justification for a change already under way.

This is the only randomised controlled trial of heroin versus methadone treatment that has ever been attempted in the UK.

## Mid-1980s: Control of HIV/AIDS

The advent of HIV/AIDS in the mid- to late-1980s saw another shift in views on maintenance prescribing. Methadone maintenance was increasingly seen as an intervention that could reduce the harm from injecting drug use. The main aim became helping injectors change their behaviour by assisting them to stabilise their drug use and reduce HIV risk behaviour (e.g. the sharing of needles and syringes). It was now seen to be a public health imperative to get heroin users into treatment and to retain them in treatment for as long as possible, thus providing the opportunity to impact on risk behaviours. But, although maintenance was back on the agenda, it was mainly with oral methadone rather than heroin.

## Mid-1990s: Prescribing Heroin to Reduce Crime

More recently, the perception of the problem has changed again. Problem heroin use is now seen by the UK government mainly as a drug-related crime issue.

The policy shift began during the first term of the Labour government after the 1997 general election. In his introduction to the White Paper *Tackling Drugs to Build a Better Britain*, the Prime Minister Tony Blair wrote of the need to 'break once and for all the vicious cycle of drugs and crime which wrecks lives and threatens communities'. The UK's first Anti Drug Coordinator (or 'drug czar'), appointed in 1997, echoed the theme in his *First Annual Report and National Plan*—the aim of which was 'to rid our society of the cycle of drugs and crime'.

The policy had several premises: crime is a key concern for communities—and a key issue for the government; a lot of crime is drug related; treatment of addicts works to reduce criminal behaviour; and drug-using criminals can be persuaded to enter treatment. Therefore, getting drug users into treatment will reduce crime. The case for expanding heroin treatment is now argued by government as one of the means for reducing drug-related acquisitive crime.

The drugs–crime focus has mellowed somewhat in the Labour government's second term—but still underpins the *Updated Drug Strategy*. Drug treatment provision is set to double between 2001 and 2008. Much of this new provision will be for methadone substitution treatment.

However, the *Updated Drug Strategy* also sets out the aim to improve access to prescribed heroin. The strategy proposes that 'all those with a clinical need for heroin prescribing will have access to it under medical provision safeguarding against the risk of seepage into the wider community'. It acknowledges the currect inconsistency in providing this treatment and pledges to spend money on it. Subsequently in May 2003, the National Treatment Agency for Substance Misuse (NTA) issued guidance on prescribing injectable heroin.

# The Evils of Heroin Are Exaggerated

*Jacob Sullum*

In the following article Jacob Sullum contends that heroin has a bad reputation because of a long tradition of antidrug propaganda. He writes that the truth about heroin is that it is neither irresistible nor inescapable and that some of those who have developed a daily habit manage to stop using the drug without professional help. Sullum says that only a small percentage of the U.S. population has used heroin and very few have become addicted to the drug. He also argues that addiction is different from physical dependence because addiction involves a psychological component. Many heroin users are only physically dependent on the drug and are able to overcome the uncomfortable but not debilitating withdrawal symptoms. Sullum also notes that the prohibition of heroin has led to serious social problems. For example, the legal restrictions on injection equipment encourage needle sharing, which in turn spreads diseases such as AIDS and hepatitis. Jacob Sullum is a senior editor for *Reason* magazine, a monthly publication that covers politics and culture.

In 1992 *The New York Times* carried a frontpage story about a successful businessman who happened to be a regular heroin user. It began: "He is an executive in a company in New York, lives in a condo on the Upper East Side of Manhattan, drives an expensive car, plays tennis in the Hamptons and vacations with his wife in Europe and the Caribbean. But unknown to office colleagues, friends, and most of his family, the man is also a longtime heroin user. He says he finds heroin relaxing and pleasurable and has seen no reason to stop using it until the woman he recently married insisted that he do so. 'The drug is an enhancement of my life,' he said. 'I see it as similar to a guy coming home and having a drink of alcohol. Only alcohol has never done it for me.'"

The *Times* noted that "nearly everything about the 44-year-old executive . . . seems to fly in the face of widely held perceptions about heroin users." The reporter who wrote the story and his editors seemed uncomfortable with contradicting official anti-drug propaganda, which depicts heroin use as incompatible with a satisfying, productive life. The headline read, "Executive's Secret Struggle With Heroin's Powerful Grip," which sounds more like a cautionary tale than a success story. And the *Times* hastened to add that heroin users "are flirting with disaster." It conceded that "heroin does not damage the organs as, for instance, heavy alcohol use does." But it cited the risk of arrest, overdose, AIDS, and hepatitis—without noting that all of these risks are created or exacerbated by prohibition.

The general thrust of the piece was: Here is a privileged man who is tempting fate by messing around with a very dangerous drug. He may have escaped disaster so far, but unless he quits he will probably end up dead or in prison.

That is not the way the businessman saw his situation. He said he had decided to give up heroin only because his wife did not approve of the habit. "In my heart," he said, "I really don't feel there's anything wrong with using heroin. But there doesn't seem to be anyway in the world I can persuade my wife to grant me this space in our relationship. I don't want to lose her, so I'm making this effort."

## Addiction Is Misperceived

Judging from the "widely held perceptions about heroin users" mentioned by the *Times*, that effort was bound to fail. The conventional view of heroin, which powerfully shapes the popular understanding of addiction, is nicely summed up in the journalist Martin Booth's 1996 history of opium. "Addiction is the compulsive taking of drugs which have such a hold over the addict he or she cannot stop using them without suffering severe symptoms and even death," he writes. "Opiate dependence . . . is as fundamental to an addict's existence as food and water, a physio-chemical fact: an addict's body is chemically reliant upon its drug for opiates actually alter the body's chemistry so it cannot function properly without being periodically primed. A hunger for the drug forms when the quantity in the bloodstream falls below a certain level. . . . Fail to feed the body and it deteriorates and may die from drug starvation." Booth also declares that "everyone . . . is a potential addict"; that "addiction can start with the very first dose"; and that "with continued use addiction is a certainty."

Booth's description is wrong or grossly misleading in every particular. To understand why is to recognize the fallacies underlying a reductionist, drug-centered view of addiction in which chemicals force themselves on people—a view that skeptics such as the maverick psychiatrist Thomas Szasz and the psychologist Stanton Peele have long questioned. The idea that a drug can compel the person who consumes it to continue consuming it is one of the most important beliefs underlying the war on drugs, because this power makes possible all the other evils to which drug use supposedly leads.

## Anti-Drug Propaganda

When Martin Booth tells us that anyone can be addicted to heroin, that it may take just one dose, and that it will certainly happen to you if you're foolish enough to repeat the experiment, he is drawing on a long tradition of anti-drug propaganda. As the sociologist Harry G. Levine has shown, the original model for such warnings was not heroin or opium but alcohol. "The idea that drugs are inherently addicting," Levine wrote in 1978, "was first systematically worked out for alcohol and then extended to other substances. Long before opium was popularly accepted as addicting, alcohol was so regarded." The dry crusaders of the 19th and early 20th centuries taught that every tippler was a potential drunkard, that a glass of beer was the first step on the road to ruin, and that repeated use of distilled spirits made addiction virtually inevitable. Today, when a kitchen wrecked by a skinny model wielding a frying pan is supposed to symbolize the havoc caused by a snort of heroin, similar assumptions about opiates are even more widely held, and they likewise are based more on faith than facts.

## Withdrawal Symptoms Are Exaggerated

Beginning early in the 20th century, Stanton Peele notes, heroin "came to be seen in American society as the nonpareil drug of addiction—as leading inescapably from even the most casual contact to an intractable dependence, withdrawal from which was traumatic and unthinkable for the addict." According to this view, reflected in Booth's gloss and other popular portrayals, the potentially fatal agony of withdrawal is the gun that heroin holds to the addict's head. These accounts greatly exaggerate both the severity and the importance of withdrawal symptoms.

Heroin addicts who abruptly stop using the drug commonly report flu-like symptoms, which may include chills, sweating, runny nose and eyes, muscular aches, stomach cramps, nausea, diarrhea, or headaches. While certainly unpleasant, the experience is not life threatening. Indeed, addicts who have developed tolerance (needing higher doses to achieve the same effect) often voluntarily undergo withdrawal so they can begin using heroin again at a lower dose, thereby reducing the cost of their habit. Another sign that fear of withdrawal symptoms is not the essence of addiction is the fact that heroin users commonly drift in and out of their habits, going through periods of abstinence and returning to the drug long after any physical discomfort has faded away. Indeed, the observation that detoxification is not tantamount to overcoming an addiction, that addicts typically will try repeatedly before successfully kicking the habit, is a commonplace of drug treatment.

More evidence that withdrawal has been overemphasized as a motivation for using opiates comes from patients who take narcotic painkillers over extended periods of time. Like heroin addicts, they develop "physical dependence" and experience withdrawal symptoms when they stop taking the drugs. But studies conducted during the last two decades [in the 1980s and 1990s] have consistently found that patients in pain who receive opioids (opiates or synthetics with similar effects) rarely become addicted.

## Physical Dependence Is Not Addiction

Pain experts emphasize that physical dependence should not be confused with addiction, which requires a psychological component: a persistent desire to use the substance for its mood-altering effects. Critics have long complained that unreasonable fears about narcotic addiction discourage adequate pain treatment. In 1989 Charles Schuster, then director of the National Institute on Drug Abuse, confessed, "We have been so effective in warning the medical establishment and the public in general about the inappropriate use of opiates that we have endowed these drugs with a mysterious power to enslave that is overrated."

Although popular perceptions lag behind, the point made by pain specialists—that "physical dependence" is not the same as addiction—is now widely accepted by professionals who deal with drug problems. But under the heroin-based model that prevailed until the 1970s, tolerance and withdrawal symptoms were considered the hallmarks of addiction. By this standard, drugs such as nicotine and cocaine were not truly addictive; they were merely "habituating." That distinction proved untenable, given the difficulty that people often had in giving up substances that were not considered addictive.

## Defining Substance Dependence

Having hijacked the term addiction, which in its original sense referred to any strong habit, psychiatrists ultimately abandoned it in favor of substance dependence. "The essential feature of Substance Dependence," according to the American Psychiatric Association, "is a cluster of cognitive, behavioral, and physiological symptoms indicating that the individual continues use of the substance despite significant substance-related problems. . . . Neither tolerance nor withdrawal is necessary or sufficient for a diagnosis of Substance Dependence." Instead, the condition is defined as "a maladaptive pattern of substance use" involving at least three of seven features. In addition to tolerance and withdrawal, these include using more of the drug than intended; trying unsuccessfully to cut back; spending a lot of time getting the drug, using it, or recovering from its effects; giving up or reducing important social, occupational, or recreational activities because of drug use; and continuing use even while recognizing drug-related psychological or physical problems.

One can quibble with these criteria, especially since they are meant to be applied not by the drug user himself but by a government-licensed expert with whose judgment he may disagree. The possibility of such a conflict is all the more troubling because the evaluation may be involuntary (the result of an arrest, for example) and may have implications for the drug user's freedom. More fundamentally, classifying substance dependence as a "mental disorder" to be treated by medical doctors suggests that drug abuse is a disease, something that happens to people rather than something that people do. Yet it is clear from the description that we are talking about a pattern of behavior. Addiction is not simply a matter of introducing a chemical into someone's body, even if it is done often enough to create tolerance and withdrawal symptoms. Conversely, someone who takes a steady dose of a drug and who can stop using it without physical distress may still be addicted to it.

Even if addiction is not a physical compulsion, perhaps some drug experiences are so alluring that people find it impossible to resist them. Certainly that is heroin's reputation, encapsulated in the title of a 1972 book: *It's So Good, Don't Even Try It Once.*

## Heroin Is Not Irresistible

The fact that heroin use is so rare—involving, according to the government's data, something like 0.2 percent of the U.S. population in 2001—suggests that its appeal is much more limited than we've been led to believe. If heroin really is "so good," why does it have such a tiny share of the illegal drug market? Marijuana is more than 45 times as popular. The National Household Survey on Drug Abuse indicates that about 3 million Americans have used heroin in their lifetimes; of them, 15 percent had used it in the last year, 4 percent in the last month. These numbers suggest that the vast majority of heroin users either never become addicted or, if they do, manage to give the drug up. A survey of high school seniors found that 1 percent had used heroin in the previous year, while 0.1 percent had used it on 20 or more days in the previous month. Assuming that daily use is a reasonable proxy for opiate addiction, one in 10 of the students who had taken heroin in the last year might have qualified as addicts. These are not the sort of numbers you'd expect for a drug that's irresistible.

True, these surveys exclude certain groups in which heroin use is more common and in which a larger percentage of users probably could be described as addicts. The household survey misses people living on the street, in prisons, and in residential drug treatment programs, while the high school survey leaves out truants and dropouts. But even for the entire population of heroin users, the estimated addiction rates do not come close to matching heroin's reputation. A 1976 study by the drug researchers Leon G. Hunt and Carl D. Chambers estimated there were 3 or 4 million heroin users in the United States, perhaps 10 percent of them addicts. "Of all active heroin users," Hunt and Chambers wrote, "a large majority are not addicts: they are not physically or socially dysfunctional; they are not daily users and they do not seem to require treatment." A 1994 study based on data from the National Comorbidity Survey estimated that 23 percent of heroin users ever experience substance dependence.

## THE HISTORY OF DRUGS

# The Difference Between Pure Heroin and Street Heroin

*Pure heroin is relatively safe and is quite different from street heroin, which has various substances added to it.*

Pure heroin (diamorphine) is used in some countries as a way of killing pain after accidents, after surgical operations, or when someone is suffering from pain caused by an illness such as cancer. It is one of the strongest painkillers available. Pure heroin is not, in itself, very harmful. According to some studies the nicotine in cigarettes is a more powerfully addictive drug and alcohol does much more long-term damage. The heroin taken by people who are dependent on the drug, however, is very different from clean, pure heroin.

The strength of heroin varies considerably, from about five to 50 percent purity or more. It is the substances that are added to heroin that cause much of the death and injury linked to the drug. Addicts always run the risk of taking so much that their breathing is slowed, sometimes so much that they die. This overdosing is usually caused by the fact that the user does not know exactly what has been mixed with the heroin, and how pure the drug that they are smoking or injecting actually is.

Mark Pownall, *Drugs, the Complete Story: Heroin.* Austin, TX: Steck-Vaughn, 1992, p. 8.

## Comparing Heroin with Alcohol and Nicotine

The comparable rate for alcohol in that study was 15 percent, which seems to support the idea that heroin is more addictive: A larger percentage of the people who try it become heavy users, even though it's harder to get. At the same time, the fact that using heroin is illegal, expensive, risky, inconvenient, and almost universally condemned means that the people who nevertheless choose to do it repeatedly will tend to differ from people who choose to drink. They will be especially attracted to heroin's effects, the associated lifestyle, or both. In other words, heroin users are a self-selected group, less representative of the general population than alcohol users are, and they may be more inclined from the outset to form strong attachments to the drug.

The same study found that 32 percent of tobacco users had experienced substance dependence. Figures like that one are the basis for the claim that nicotine is "more addictive than heroin." After all, cigarette smokers typically go through a pack or so a day, so they're under the influence of nicotine every waking moment. Heroin users typically do not use their drug even once a day. Smokers offended by this comparison are quick to point out that they function fine, meeting their responsibilities at work and home despite their habit. This, they assume, is impossible for heroin users. Examples like the businessman described by *The New York Times* indicate otherwise.

## Cigarettes Harder to Give Up

Still, it's true that nicotine's psychoactive effects are easier to reconcile with the requirements of everyday life than heroin's are. Indeed, nicotine can enhance concentration and improve performance on certain tasks. So one important reason why most cigarette smokers consume their drug throughout the day is that they can do so without running into trouble. And because they're used to smoking in so many different settings, they may find nicotine harder to give up than a drug they use only with certain people in secret. In one survey, 57 percent of drug users entering a Canadian treatment program said giving up their problem substance (not necessarily heroin) would be easier than giving up cigarettes. In another survey, 36 heroin users entering treatment were asked to compare their strongest cigarette urge to their strongest heroin urge. Most said the heroin urge was stronger, but two said the cigarette urge was, and 11 rated the two urges about the same.

In a sense, nicotine's compatibility with a wide range of tasks makes it more addictive than alcohol or heroin. But this is not the sort of thing people usually have in mind when they worry about addiction. Indeed, if it weren't for the health effects of smoking (and the complaints of bystanders exposed to the smoke), nicotine addiction probably would be seen as no big deal, just as caffeine addiction is. As alternative sources of nicotine that do not involve smoking (gum, patches, inhalers, beverages, lozenges, oral snuff) become popular not just as aids in quitting but as long-term replacements, it will be interesting to see whether they will be socially accepted. Once the health risks are dramatically reduced or eliminated, will daily consumption of nicotine still be viewed as shameful and declasse, as a disease to be treated or a problem to be overcome? Perhaps so, if addiction per se is the issue. But not if it's the medical, social, and psychological consequences of addiction that really matter.

## Problems with Prohibition

To a large extent, regular heroin use also can be separated from the terrible consequences that have come to be associated with it. Because of prohibition, users face the risk of arrest and imprisonment, the handicap of a criminal record, and the violence associated with the black market. The artificially high price of heroin, perhaps 40 or 50 times what it would otherwise cost, may lead to heavy debts, housing problems, poor nutrition, and theft. The inflated cost also encourages users to

inject the drug, a more efficient but riskier mode of administration. The legal treatment of injection equipment, including
restrictions on distribution and penalties for possession, encourages needle sharing, which spreads diseases such as AIDS
and hepatitis. The unreliable quality and unpredictable purity
associated with the black market can lead to poisoning and
accidental overdoses.

Without prohibition, then, a daily heroin habit would be far
less burdensome and hazardous. Heroin itself is much less
likely to kill a user than the reckless combination of heroin with
other depressants, such as alcohol or barbiturates. The federal
government's Drug Abuse Warning Network counted 4,820
mentions of heroin or morphine (which are indistinguishable in
the blood) by medical examiners in 1999. Only 438 of these
deaths (9 percent) were listed as directly caused by an overdose of the opiate. Three-quarters of the deaths were caused by
heroin/morphine in combination with other drugs. Provided the
user avoids such mixtures, has access to a supply of reliable
purity, and follows sanitary injection procedures, the health
risks of long-term opiate consumption are minimal.

## Heroin Addicts Can Recover Naturally

The comparison between heroin and nicotine is also instruc-
tive when it comes to the role of drug treatment. Although
many smokers have a hard time quitting, those who succeed
generally do so on their own. Surprisingly, the same may be
true of heroin addicts. In the early 1960s, based on records
kept by the Federal Bureau of Narcotics, sociologist Charles
Winick concluded that narcotic addicts tend to "mature out" of
the habit in their 30s. He suggested that "addiction may be a
self limiting process for perhaps two-thirds of addicts." Subsequent researchers have questioned Winick's assumptions, and
other studies have come up with lower estimates. But it's clear
that "natural recovery" is much more common than the public has been led to believe.

In a 1974 study of Vietnam veterans, only 12 percent of those who were addicted to heroin in Vietnam took up the habit again during the three years after their return to the United States. (This was not because they couldn't find heroin; half of them used it at least once after their return, generally without becoming addicted again.) Those who had undergone treatment (half of the group) were just as likely to be re-addicted as those who had not. Since those with stronger addictions were more likely to receive treatment, this does not necessarily mean that treatment was useless, but it clearly was not a prerequisite for giving up heroin.

Despite its reputation, then, heroin is neither irresistible nor inescapable. Only a very small share of the population ever uses it, and a large majority of those who do never become addicted. Even within the minority who develop a daily habit, most manage to stop using heroin, often without professional intervention. Yet heroin is still perceived as the paradigmatic voodoo drug, ineluctably turning its users into zombies who must obey its commands.

# OxyContin Drug Abuse

*James A. Inciardi and Jennifer L. Goode*

OxyContin is a narcotic painkiller that was released onto the market in 1996 and was considered a breakthrough in pain management. The active ingredient in OxyContin is oxycodone, a semisynthetic opioid that has been successfully used in numerous pain medications for the past one hundred years. In this selection James A. Inciardi and Jennifer L. Goode explain that OxyContin is different from other pain medications because it does not contain aspirin or acetaminophen and it has a timed-release formula that provides continuous pain relief for up to twelve hours. The authors say that OxyContin has been heavily criticized over the last few years due to its potential for addiction and abuse. Indeed, users are injecting and snorting the dissolved tablets or crushing and eating them for the drug's powerful effects.

The authors explain that OxyContin is being illegally diverted in several ways, including illegal sales by physicians and pharmacists and thefts from pharmacies and pharmaceutical warehouses. People are also defrauding the Medicaid system by purchasing a bottle of OxyContin for a price as low as three dollars and selling it on the black market for as much as eight thousand dollars. Inciardi and Goode say that despite the avalanche of media attention the drug has received, abuse of OxyContin is still far from being epidemic.

James A. Inciardi is a professor in the Department of Sociology and Criminal Justice at the University of Delaware as

James A. Inciardi and Jennifer L. Goode, "Oxycontin and Prescription Drug Abuse," *Consumers' Research Magazine*, vol. 86, July 2003, pp. 17–22. Copyright © 2003 by Consumers' Research, Inc. Reproduced by permission.

well as director of the University's Center for Drug and Alcohol Studies. Jennifer L. Goode is a research specialist at the Center for Drug and Alcohol Studies.

Since OxyContin was first introduced to the market in early 1996, it has been hailed as a breakthrough in pain management. The medication is unique in that its time-release formula allows patients to enjoy continuous, long-term relief from moderate to severe pain. For many patients who had suffered for years from chronic pain, it gave them relief from suffering. But during the past three years [2000–2003] OxyContin has received a substantial amount of negative attention—not for its medicinal effects, but for its addiction liability and abuse potential.

## Oxycodone Is Active Ingredient

The active ingredient in OxyContin is "oxycodone," a drug that has been used for the treatment of pain for almost 100 years. Oxycodone is a semi-synthetic narcotic analgesic [opioid painkiller] most often prescribed for moderate to severe pain, chronic pain syndromes, and terminal cancers. When used correctly under a physician's supervision, oxycodone can be highly effective in the management of pain, and there are scores of oxycodone products on the market—in various strengths and forms. Popular brands include Percocet and Percodan; Roxicet and Roxicodone; and Endocet, OxyIR, and Tylox, to name but a few. However, no oxycodone product has generated as much attention as OxyContin.

Produced by the Stamford, Connecticut-based pharmaceutical company, Purdue Pharma L.P., OxyContin is unique because unlike other oxycodone products that typically contain aspirin or acetaminophen to increase or lengthen their potency, OxyContin is a single entity product that can provide up to 12 hours of continuous pain relief. Tablets are available in

10-, 20-, 40-, and 80-milligram doses. The company also introduced a 160-milligram dose in July 2000 for its opioid-tolerant patients, only later to withdraw it from the market amidst controversy over its alleged abuse.

## The "Black Box" Warning

When the clinical trials for OxyContin were reviewed by the Food and Drug Administration [FDA], the drug was demonstrated to be an effective analgesic in individuals with chronic, moderate-to-severe pain. Yet it was also judged by the FDA to carry a substantial risk of abuse because of its properties as a narcotic. As a result, OxyContin was approved by the FDA but placed in Schedule II of the Controlled Substances Act (CSA), which is the tightest level of control that can be placed on an approved drug for medical purposes. The placement of Oxy-Contin in Schedule II warned physicians and patients that the drug carried a high potential for abuse and that it needed to be carefully managed, particularly among those at risk for substance abuse. In addition, in the Physicians' Desk Reference and on the drug's package insert, OxyContin carries a boxed warning—more commonly known as the infamous "black box."

Importantly, this "black box," voluntarily inserted in the packaging information by Purdue Pharma in 2001, alerts potential users that taking broken, chewed, or crushed OxyContin tablets leads to rapid release and absorption of a potentially fatal dose of the drug. But even before the insertion of the "black box," drug abusers had figured out how to compromise OxyContin's controlled-release formula and set off on a powerful high by injecting or snorting dissolved tablets or by crushing and ingesting them.

Despite the numerous controls and warnings required by the FDA, OxyContin has been a major economic success for Purdue Pharma, accounting for some 80% of the company's total business. Prescriptions have risen steadily since the drug's introduction, as the number of prescriptions dispensed increased 20-fold from 1996 through 2000. More than 7.2 million prescriptions were dispensed in 2001 and retail sales totaled more than $1.45 billion, representing a 41% increase in sales between 2000 and 2001 alone. Retail sales increased again in 2002, topping $1.59 billion. In terms of dollar amount, OxyContin now ranks the highest in retail sales of all brand-name controlled substances. Federal regulators, however, are put off by these numbers, and focus on the diversion of OxyContin to illegal markets, and reports of OxyContin abuse and overdose deaths.

## Illegal Marketplace

Prescription drug diversion involves the unlawful movement of regulated pharmaceuticals from legal sources to the illegal marketplace, and OxyContin's attractiveness to drug abusers has resulted in its diversion in a number of ways. The major mechanisms include the illegal sale of prescriptions by physicians and pharmacists; "doctor shopping" by individuals who visit numerous physicians to obtain multiple prescriptions; the theft, forgery, or alteration of prescriptions by patients; robberies and thefts from pharmacies and pharmaceutical warehouses; and thefts of samples from physicians' offices as well as thefts of institutional drug supplies by health-care workers. In all likelihood, OxyContin has been diverted through all of these routes.

Diversion has also occurred by means of fraud, particularly through the abuse of medical insurance programs, a phenomenon observed and investigated most often in a number of rural communities. Medicaid fraud, for example, presents an inexpensive mechanism for abusing drugs and oftentimes an easy route to a lucrative enterprise. For example, a Medicaid patient may pay only $3 for a bottle of a hundred 80-milligram OxyContin tablets. In areas where employment and money are scarce resources, the temptation to sell some of the pills for the going "street price" of $1 per milligram provides an opportunity to earn money. In this example, the $3 bottle from the pharmacy can net the patient up to $8,000 on the illegal market.

## Physicians Arrested

Just one corrupt physician, pharmacist, health-care worker, or other employee in the health-care field can have a significant impact on the availability of the product as well. For example, before he was arrested in 2002, a Pennsylvania pharmacist had illegally sold hundreds of thousands of painkillers, including OxyContin, over a three-year period. He made $900,000 on his transactions (only to lose it all in the stock market). Although he operated an independent neighborhood pharmacy, he was reportedly the state's third-largest purchaser of Oxy-Contin. Similarly, a number of physicians in Eastern Kentucky were arrested in 2003 for a variety of diversion schemes. One saw as many as 150 patients each day, writing narcotic prescriptions for them after a visit of less than three minutes each. Another traded painkillers for sex with female patients whom he had addicted to narcotics. A third opened an office in a shopping mall where he generated prescriptions—one after another—almost as quickly as he could write them.

How much diversion of OxyContin actually occurs is impossible to calculate, because there is not a single national reporting system on pharmaceutical diversion. Nevertheless, some data are available which at least suggest the extent of OxyContin diversion, relative to other drugs of abuse, including narcotic painkillers. In a 2001 survey of 34 police agencies with pharmaceutical diversion units, for example, a total of 5,802 cases of diversion (of any drug) were reported during the calendar year. The reporting agencies were asked to indicate which drugs were most commonly diverted, and in how many cases each was investigated. The most commonly diverted pharmaceutical drug was hydrocodone (Vicodin, Lortab, and similar narcotic analgesics), noted in 31% of the total cases.

This was followed by oxycodone in 12% of the cases, and al-prazolam (Xanax) in 6% of the cases. Of the 701 cases involving an oxycodone product, 416 were OxyContin. Overall, Oxy-Contin was represented in only 7% of the drug diversions, a rather small proportion given the attention the drug has received. In addition, the data documented that the diversion of OxyContin was part of a much broader pattern of prescription-drug diversion. That is, in the great majority of cases in which OxyContin had been diverted, a wide spectrum of other drugs were being diverted at the same time.

## Who Abuses OxyContin?

Although there are several sources of national data on drug abuse that have been operating for decades, the collection of specific data on OxyContin abuse is quite recent. In the Monitoring the Future Survey, a government-sponsored study of drug abuse among high school students and young adults that has been conducted annually since 1975, the collection of information on OxyContin began only in 2002—and this was initiated at the request of Purdue Pharma. The 2002 survey found that 4% of 12th graders, 3% of 10th graders, and 1.3% of 8th graders had used OxyContin at least once during the past year. Interestingly, the use of Vicodin (a brand of hydrocodone) in [2003] was at least double that of OxyContin—9.6% for 12th graders, 6.9% for 10th graders, and 2.5% for 8th graders. In the 2001 National Household Survey on Drug Abuse, another government survey conducted annually, only "lifetime use" (at least once in a person's lifetime "to get high") data were collected for OxyContin. For persons ages 12 and over, less than one-half of 1% reported ever using OxyContin to get high.

The Drug Enforcement Administration started actively collecting and analyzing data from medical examiners in an attempt to establish the extent of the OxyContin problem. Medical examiner reports from 2000–2001 from 32 states reflected that 949 deaths were associated with oxycodone, of which almost half (49%) were "likely" related to OxyContin. Because there are a multitude of oxycodone products on the market, it is impossible to determine the specific brand of drug found in a cadaver. Nevertheless, out of the 949 deaths, DEA reported that 146 were "OxyContin verified," while another 318 were "OxyContin likely." To make things even more complicated, the majority of the toxicological analyses reported multiple-drug use, suggesting that the death may have been the result of an overdose induced by a combination of substances, not just oxycodone by itself. When taking all of these factors into consideration, it is very difficult to establish a direct link between OxyContin and cause of death.

## OxyContin Abuse May Be Increasing

OxyContin abuse first surfaced in rural Maine during the late 1990s, and soon after spread down the east coast and Ohio Valley, and then into rural Appalachia. Communities in western Virginia, eastern Kentucky, West Virginia, and southern Ohio were especially hard hit, and a number of factors characteristic of these areas seem to correlate with their apparent high rates of abuse. In northern Maine and rural Appalachia, for example, there are aspects of the culture that are markedly different from those in other parts of the country. Many of the communities are quite small and isolated, often situated in the mountains and "hollers" a considerable distance from major towns and highways. As a result, many of the usual street drugs are simply not available. Instead, locals make do with resources already on hand, like prescription drugs. In addition, isolation impacts heavily on options for amenities and entertainment. Many substance-abuse treatment clients in these rural areas have told their counselors that they started using drugs because of boredom.

Many adults in these rural areas tend to suffer from chronic illnesses and pain syndromes, born out of hard lives of manual labor in perilous professions—coal mining, logging, fishing, and other blue-collar industries which often result in serious and debilitating injuries. As a result, a disproportionately high segment of the population lives on strong painkillers. The use of pain pills evolves into a kind of coping mechanism, and the practice of self-medication becomes a way for life for many. As such, the use of narcotic analgesics has become normalized and integrated into the local culture.

Data suggest that the abuse of OxyContin may be escalating in certain areas. For example, the number of patients in Kentucky seeking treatment for oxycodone addiction increased 163% from 1998 to 2000. While OxyContin is not necessarily always the cause, officials there say that it is one of the most widely abused oxycodone products. Crime statistics seem to support the claim, as Kentucky is one of the leading states for OxyContin-related crimes. Between January 2000 and June 2001 alone, 69 of the state's 1,000 pharmacies reported OxyContin-related break-ins.

## Treatment Admissions for OxyContin Increased

Drug treatment admissions from several states may also offer evidence to support a growing trend in OxyContin abuse. Programs in Pennsylvania, Kentucky, and Virginia have reported that 50% to 90% of newly admitted patients identified OxyContin as their drug of choice. Figures obtained by DEA from the American Methadone Treatment Association also suggest an increase in the number of patients admitted for OxyContin abuse. Moreover, according to the Maine Office of Substance Abuse, the number of narcotics-related treatment admissions (excluding heroin) increased from 73 in 1995 to 762 in 2001. While OxyContin cannot take all of the blame, officials say it is nonetheless a major contributor and also point out that opiate-based prescription drugs in general outpaced the percentage increases for all "other" types of drugs in the state.

Treatment admissions for these drugs increased 78% from 1998 to 1999 (199 to 355) and another 47% from 1999 through September 2000 (355 to 521), which suggests a possible increase in OxyContin use.

A separate study conducted by Maine's Substance Abuse Services Commission and the Maine Office of Substance Abuse found that treatment admissions for narcotic abuse increased 500% since 1995, and that opiate-related arrests constituted more than 40% of the Maine Drug Enforcement Agency's caseload. The study, commissioned because of the publicity the state received for being one of the first to identify OxyContin abuse, analyzed several aspects of prescription opiate abuse. The study linked the use of narcotics with increased rates of crime, emergency medical treatment, and outbreaks of hepatitis C. While OxyContin was not the only opiate abused in the state at the time, it constituted the centerpiece of the study results published in *Alcoholism & Drug Abuse Weekly.*

Based on these and similar reports in a few other states, it has been suggested in numerous media outlets that the abuse of OxyContin is on the rise, and that its popularity is rapidly spreading beyond the rural East Coast to other parts of the United States. At the same time, however, there is also concern that the media have played an integral role in boosting the drug's popularity.

## The Media Frenzy

Media outlets in Maine began reporting on OxyContin abuse in early 2000. The *Bangor Daily News*, for example, ran several features which included information not only about the properties of the drug, but also about how to compromise its time-release mechanism, the tactics of diversion that people were using to obtain the drug (including Medicaid fraud), and the concerns of the medical profession about the potential for abusing the drug. In addition, numerous examples of alleged OxyContin-related crimes were described in detail.

Media coverage changed dramatically after Kentucky's sensational "Operation OxyFest 2001," when more than 100 law enforcement officers from numerous jurisdictions worked together to arrest 207 OxyContin users and dealers throughout the state. A blitz of national media coverage followed. The Associated Press, *Time*, *Newsweek*, the *New York Times*, and other media giants, as well as local newspapers across the nation, all ran alarming stories about the potentially lethal and dangerous new drug. Much of the initial coverage of OxyContin seemed to follow a similar formula: It started off with the personal tale of a chronically ill patient for whom OxyContin had suddenly made life worth living, followed by a contrasting tale of a lowly, depraved junkie who had become a slave to the drug, all the while littering the piece with both information and misinformation about the drug. Headlines screamed about OxyContin-related crimes, including pharmacy break-ins and terrifying accounts of elderly patients' homes being invaded and raided for the drug. Some stories of robberies appeared in local media outlets, only to be followed by a string of copycat attempts. There were numerous stories of physicians who ran "pill mills" to feed the addiction of their clients, and contrasting stories of other doctors who had been scared off from prescribing the drug. There were numerous reports of pharmacies that had stopped stocking the drug for fear of inviting crime.

## Attention to OxyContin Is Overblown

It would appear that, although the abuse of OxyContin is indeed real, it is just one of many drugs that are abused by individuals whose drug-taking and drug-seeking behaviors focus on prescription painkillers. It also appears that the media stories may have contributed to shifting OxyContin abuse from a regional problem to a national problem. Clearly, OxyContin abuse is anything but an "epidemic." Nevertheless, all of the attention given to OxyContin has prompted U.S. government involvement. In response to the heightened awareness of Oxy-

Contin abuse and diversion, the DEA launched its own comprehensive plan to prevent the illegal distribution of the product. Its broad goals include enforcement and intelligence; regulatory and administrative authority; industry cooperation; and awareness, education and outreach initiatives. Industry cooperation is an integral part of the plan, including encouraging Purdue to adopt a balanced marketing plan. As recently as January 2003, the FDA sent Purdue a letter contending that the company improperly disclosed information on OxyContin's risks, including a "particularly disturbing" ad that ran in the November issue of *JAMA* (the *Journal of the American Medical Association*). In response, Purdue has pledged that all future advertisements will balance information about the benefits and risks of the product, as required by the federal Food, Drug and Cosmetic Act.

## Outsmarting Drug Abusers

There have also been calls to reformulate the drug, to make it more difficult for abusers to compromise its time-release mechanism. Purdue has pursued alternative formulas, but success has been elusive thus far. Clinical trials found that when naloxone, a narcotic blocker, was added to OxyContin, it sometimes blocked pain relief for patients who ingested the tablets correctly. The company is pursuing an alternate approach by shifting from a tablet to a capsule that contains similar beads of the oxycodone combined with naltrexone, another narcotic blocker. If taken correctly, only the OxyContin beads would dissolve in the system, but if an abuser were to crush the pill, he would crush and activate the naltrexone, therefore masking the drug's effects. The company said complete testing could take as long as five years. Even if this is accomplished, drug abusers are clever people, and will likely compromise the new formulation in due course.

In the meantime, Purdue has launched its own public relations offensive. Among the initiatives, it has created educational and outreach materials, including a series of print and television ads and "Painfully Obvious," a program that provides resources to educate parents, teachers, and students about the dangers of prescription drug abuse.

Despite the bad press and pressure from the government, the success of OxyContin has not faltered. Only time will tell if the success will be short-lived or if the negative attention will slowly start to chip away at product confidence. In the meantime, those who use it correctly will continue to enjoy consistent pain relief, while those who abuse it will surely continue to inflict pain on the company, law enforcement, the community, and themselves.

# Central Asia's Opiate Problem

*Aram Roston*

Central Asia is a major producer of opium and heroin. In the following selection writer Aram Roston says that authorities estimate that Afghanistan alone produces three-quarters of the world's heroin. According to Roston, severe poverty forces countries such as Afghanistan and Tajikistan to grow opium poppies in order to survive, and warlords there manipulate the drug trade to consolidate their power. Roston explains that the poppy fields in Central Asia are well established in the most fertile areas, where factory workers extract the opium from the flowers and carefully grade it for purity. Roston says that international efforts to curb the opium trade in Central Asia have been unsuccessful because of widespread corruption in the unstable countries in this region. Further, until the terrorist attacks of September 11, 2001, the United States had an extremely hands-off drug policy in Central Asia. Roston says that the production of opium and heroin continues to flourish in Central Asia. Aram Roston is a writer who has worked as a New York City police reporter, an investigative producer at ABC News, and as a CNN correspondent.

In Khujand, Tajikistan, when someone shows up with a new Mercedes or Audi or Jaguar, the joke on the street is that people don't ask how much money it cost. They ask how many kilos it cost.

As the drug trade has saturated Afghanistan over the past

decade [1990–2000], trafficking routes have been carved through the brittle landscape of the Central Asian nations to the north, like Tajikistan. Increases in crime, corruption and addiction have followed, while repressive governments have used the fight against narcotics as another tool to crush political opponents.

One tour of the heroin route can begin in northern Afghanistan, where organized religious fanatics produce the drugs, and continue north through Tajikistan, where organized criminals of a more familiar stripe take over. A good place to start the tour is the city of Taloqan, where the elegant tree-lined boulevards and the bustling bazaar belie its role as a fiercely contested strategic point in the north. According to one United Nations diplomat, about two tons of heroin flow through Taloqan each month. The city was a prize taken by the Taliban from the Northern Alliance in 2000, and then, this past November [2001], it was recaptured by the Northern Alliance in its US-backed blitzkrieg through the country.

Nearby, UN experts say, there is a group of warehouses with enough stockpiled heroin to export a hundred tons a year for the next three years. According to a Western diplomat familiar with the drug trade, when Taloqan fell [in the] fall [of 2001] the owners of the heroin warehouses reached a new accommodation with the incoming conquerors, switching sides even before the door had swung shut behind the exiting Taliban. The warehouses "are not destroyed, they are just waiting."

## Poverty Makes Drug Production Necessary

In Afghanistan, poverty has made drug production necessary for survival, and warlords have used it to consolidate their power. Virtually the entire economy is black market, aside from aid money. The legal exports are worth approximately $80 million, according to the CIA's World Fact Book: mostly carpets, dried fruit, nuts. The opium crop, at rock-bottom prices in Afghan markets, is worth at least $120 million, based on UN estimates of $30 a kilogram in February 2000. Since then, the wholesale price has jumped tenfold. The true value of the exported drugs, once they hit the streets in Moscow, Amsterdam, Geneva, London or New York, is estimated at up to $100 billion.

Unlike in Colombia, Afghanistan's drugs aren't grown high in tree-covered hills; instead, the poppy is cultivated more overtly in the only really fertile areas the country has: the bottom land along rivers, in Badakshan, Nangarhar, Kandahar, Oruzgan. Then it's processed near the cities. Afghan heroin production is highly professional; the one-kilo plastic bags are stamped with the names of the factories where they are produced. One that I saw in November [2001] was stamped "999"; underneath, it said "95%. Azad private factory—The Best of All Export, Super White." "Abdur Rauf" read another, "wholesale," "Faizabad," meaning that's the city of origin. Faizabad has always been under the command of the Northern Alliance.

## Afghanistan Is a Major Opium and Heroin Producer

Afghanistan produces three-quarters of the world's opium and heroin—hundreds of tons a year. As a result, America's allies in the current global conflict, as well as its enemies, are neck-deep in the narcotics business. As the postwar gamesmanship shifts into high gear, a US official preparing for negotiations tells *The Nation*, "We're going to be dealing with people at all sorts of levels who've had involvement with the opium trade."

And that's been the flavor of the confusing war on both terror and drugs in the region. Less than a year before the Taliban's designation as the enemy in the wake of September 11, Afghanistan's brutal rulers won accolades from the West for a ban on poppy cultivation. Last May [2001] the United States announced a $43 million aid package widely seen as a reward. The ban was successful—because of the Taliban's implacable violence and a drought—but cynical, shoring up the price while allowing traffickers to unload huge stockpiles they'd built up.

In January [2002] Afghan interim leader Hamid Karzai announced a new ban on drugs, hardly a surprise as he shakes international trees for aid, but unrealistic in an Afghanistan that is nearly ungovernable and desperate for cash. The problem was that under the green thumbs of America's allies, large-scale planting had already begun when the Taliban fell. In some villages, as much as 70 percent of the acreage was sown with opium poppy instead of wheat. President Bush acknowledged in late February [2002] that the country had failed to stem drug production, but exempted the country from the cutoff in aid that ordinarily follows such a finding.

## Smuggling Routes

From Taloqan and cities like it, the smuggling route heads north along the dusty steppes, with opium and processed heroin in armed convoys passing the streams of refugees, toward the infinite informal crossing points on the 900-mile border with Tajikistan. There is the Pyanj River, where fishermen use grenades to kill carp, and beyond that the no man's land that ends with a double chain-link fence.

Across the border, the small Tajik town of Moskovsky has become one of the major transit points these days. It is separated from Afghanistan by a kilometer or so of flat, landmined terrain, guarded by underpaid Russian troops. Even after the USSR's implosion, the Russians' 201st Motorized Division stayed to protect this unlikely border, marking the territory it considers vital as a buffer. The Russians have frequent skirmishes with armed smugglers. On October 12 [2001] a group of smugglers tried to sneak across with about forty-two kilos of heroin. They were intercepted, and in the fighting, a Russian soldier and a smuggler were killed. Two weeks later there was yet another battle. This time the smugglers fled back to Afghanistan, abandoning about eighty-one kilos.

On the northern side of the Pyanj riverbank, men in leather coats, square-tipped shoes and fancy cars take over from the turbaned, bearded Afghans. They arrange for the heroin to be repacked, hidden in cars, trucks, or on mules, or smuggled by impoverished peasants.

## A Father Feels Forced to Deal in Heroin

North along this two-lane road in Tajikistan is Farhar. Last fall [2001] Davlat Ivganovich, a local driver, who used to make about $1.80 a day, couldn't find work for five months. This father of five ran into a friend, a heroin trafficker, on the street one day near his house. "I said I needed money, that was my only way out." His friend said, "Twenty dollars." He was to head up north to Khujand carrying a half-kilo packet of heroin in a bag with a flowery design. At a prearranged spot, a man would recognize him by the bag and would collect the heroin. Davlat agreed at once. "Of course I knew it was illegal, but I had to do this in order to live."

He was caught on the way. When I met him he was brought out of an unlit holding cell, a short man, disheveled and nervous. "I think my children will probably become beggars," he said, showing no emotion. He's probably right, and they are not alone. The levels of poverty here are obscene even by the standards of the former Soviet Union. The average monthly income is less than $10.

## A Smuggler's Dream

Tajikistan is still recovering from its civil war, which began as if on cue in 1992, shortly after the collapse of the Soviet Union. It claimed the lives of an estimated 60,000 people, and in a nation with a population of only 6 million, that means blood was literally splattering the countryside. In 1997 a fragile peace agreement resulted in a coalition government. The clannish makeup of this society meant that groups of warlords, once the war was done, could easily transfer their energies to smuggling. "There were structures on both sides, big shots on all sides, who were already organized," says one UN official. "That's why organized crime developed so quickly." It is a smuggler's dream, with an unstable, corrupt and weak government; mountainous, sparsely inhabited terrain; and borders impossible to police. The rise in smuggling has made the authorities' heads spin. Five years ago [in 1997] heroin was virtually unknown in the country. Last year [2001], authorities reported they'd seized almost four tons of the stuff as of November.

The drive that Davlat Ivganovich took, hugging his half-kilo of heroin in the flowery bag, follows a winding road through stunning, merciless mountains. The path is lined by checkpoints manned by Tajik security officials. Usually they want a small bribe, a dollar or so, to let the cars go on their way. It is a truism that the cars that most obviously belong to drug dealers, the snazzy, incongruous Mercedes, or even Jaguars, are the ones that are not stopped and searched; the officers have to assume that someone who can afford a car like that is too powerful to hassle.

The road climbs past a beautiful lake in territory controlled by a warlord who is, according to some officials, allied with the leader of one of the most feared terrorist groups in that part of the world, the Islamic Movement of Uzbekistan, which has been closely linked with Osama bin Laden's Al Qaeda network. The group has launched armed incursions into Tajikistan, Kyrgyzstan and Uzbekistan's Fergana Valley over the past few years. The attacks, some officials speculate, were intended to help solidify new drug-trafficking routes.

## Combating the Heroin Trade

In Tajikistan's capital, Dushanbe, Gen. Rustam Nazarov, the head of the nation's Drug Control Agency, sees his country's problems as a direct result of the troubles in Afghanistan. Asked about the difference between the sides in the conflict there, he waves his hand dismissively. The prospect of the Northern Alliance cracking down on the drug trade in a grateful token of appreciation for US aid in its victory is unlikely, Nazarov believes. The drug trade finances the Northern Alliance just as it did the Taliban. To give it up would be to give up their income. A compact man with a five o'clock shadow at 10 in the morning, he quietly sums it up: "One part of the Afghan population fights. The other side produces drugs."

So far, international efforts to combat the Central Asian heroin trade have been troubled. Nazarov's agency, funded by the UN, has a massive budget by local standards. The idea is simple: Pay police officers more to cut down on graft. The UN Office of Drug Control and Crime Prevention (UNDCCP) pays its officers about $200 a month, a livable wage (other police officers get around $15 a month). UN diplomats say the agency's massive seizures are proof that it is working. Even so, there are lingering allegations of corruption and a concern that the agency may just be rewarding a system of graft by paying high salaries to those involved.

## The United States Maintains a Hands-Off Policy

As Central Asia blossomed into one of the world's most significant drug and crime bazaars, America was barely watching, following a relatively hands-off policy in contrast to its concern with other drug-producing areas. Because of precarious security in Tajikistan, the United States has not had an embassy there since 1998. Nazarov flew to the United States himself to plead with the Drug Enforcement Administration for aid, and he says he left empty-handed. "The United States has been ignoring this region until the events of New York," he says quietly. "Until then there was an impression that Afghanistan doesn't exist for the Western world."

The region has received some antinarcotics aid through the State Department's Bureau for International Narcotics and Law Enforcement Affairs—about $11 million over three years—and from the UN, which is spending $16 million on various programs. But aid here can be more like a cluster bomb than a surgical strike, with unintended consequences. In a recent report for the Open Society Institute, chief author Nancy Lubin asks "whether the training and equipment provided by the United States and others to Central Asia has actually been used to fight drug trafficking, or to crack down on domestic political opposition," or to assist government officials and others to more effectively traffic drugs.

Matilda Bogner of Human Rights Watch in Uzbekistan, where religious opposition figures are tortured, maimed, imprisoned and executed, agrees. "Police officers will plant either a small amount of narcotics or they will plant a few bullets on someone they want to arrest." Now the DEA plans to send two agents to Tashkent, where they will be confronted with such policing tactics and may have to distinguish legitimate drug investigations from thinly veiled repression.

## Women Act as "Mules"

It is the suddenness with which heroin has penetrated this region that has shaken it so much. Antonella Deledda, the graceful Italian diplomat who heads the UN's antidrug efforts in the area, points out a startling change in the traditional fabric of life in the region—the rising role of women in the drug trade. According to one report, 30 percent of the "mules" handling narcotics in Kyrgyzstan are women, and the figure in Tajikistan may be even higher.

For many of Tajikistan's women, their journey down the heroin route ends over the passes of the Fan Mountains north of Khujand. In the badlands there, a dirt road leads past some sheep grazing on clumps of weeds, toward the only women's prison in Tajikistan. One woman shuffles near the gate, wearing a filthy chakan and slippers, and carrying a little bowl of food. There are almost 300 women here behind the dirty white walls topped with barbed wire. More than half of them are imprisoned on drug charges. They are arrested as they work their way to Russia by train or by plane, at border checkpoints or in sweeps. Peasant women have taped drug packages under their breasts, inserted them inside their vaginas or anuses, or swallowed them. One press account reports that a woman flying to Moscow from Dushanbe had swallowed more than seven kilos of the stuff: In terms of volume, that's bigger than a basketball—it's probably closer to a beach ball.

## Fight Against Narcoterrorists Is Unsuccessful

Colombia, where women have been mules for decades, might offer some lessons for this latest war in a number of ways. Until the current campaign against terror, Colombia was America's biggest military engagement, a war viewed by successive administrations solely through the prism of the drug trade, where the United States continues, to no evident effect, its fight by proxy against "narcoterrorists." The real terrorists operating out of Afghanistan made that vague term seem even more inaccurate. With the fall of the Taliban, there may be opportunities during the reconstruction to wean the economy off narcotics, but so far, victory has meant propping up a coalition of warlords, many of whom are linked to the drug business. In early February [2002] the DEA sent a contingent of agents to Afghanistan as well. They have their work cut out for them. The UN estimates that the crop planted under the friendly new Afghanistan may yield up to 2,700 metric tons of opium. It will be ready for harvest in the spring.

**acetic anhydride:** A colorless liquid with a strong, vinegar-like odor; also known as acetic oxide or acetyl oxide. It is a key precursor chemical and reagent in heroin synthesis. In illicit heroin production, acetic anhydride is the most commonly used acetylating agent in the acetylation of morphine.

**acetylation:** The key chemical process in converting morphine base to heroin.

**alkaloid:** Any of the various physiologically active, nitrogen-containing organic bases derived from plants. Common alkaloids include caffeine, cocaine, codeine, mescaline, morphine, nicotine, quinine, and strychnine.

**analgesic:** A drug that reduces pain.

**antitussive:** A preparation that reduces the severity of coughing.

**brown sugar heroin:** A common name for heroin that has the appearance of light brown, granulated sugar. It is commonly produced in Southwest Asia (Afghanistan, Pakistan, and Iran).

***chandu:*** A Hindi-Bengali term for cooked opium ("smoking opium") that is used in India and some parts of Burma.

**China White:** Southeast Asian heroin no. 4 in white powder form. It may be injected, snorted, or smoked.

**Golden Triangle:** The area of mainland Southeast Asia consisting of northeastern Burma, the highlands of northwestern Laos, and the highlands of northern Thailand. The term was popularized by Western journalists in the 1970s to designate one of the principal source areas in the world for illicit opium and its derivatives: morphine and heroin. The region's poppy cultivation area also includes northern Vietnam and the adjacent areas of southern China.

**gram:** A standard unit of weight in the metric system equal to one thousandth of a kilogram. One ounce equals 28.350 grams.

**heroin:** An addictive synthetic narcotic derived from morphine. It is also known as diacetylmorphine or diamorphine.

**heroin base:** The substance produced when morphine is mixed with acetic anhydride.

**heroin no. 3:** A smokeable form of Southeast Asian heroin that is not as highly refined as no. 4. Its color ranges from purple to tan to off-white.

**heroin no. 4:** An injectable form of highly refined heroin produced in Southeast Asia. It is also known as heroin hydrochloride or China White. It is usually a fine white powder, flakes, or crystals and may be smoked or snorted.

**heroin salt:** The addictive form of heroin, obtained after heroin base has been treated chemically.

**kilogram:** A metric unit of weight equal to one thousand grams or 2.2046 pounds.

**laudanum:** A mixture of opium and alcohol.

**mainlining:** This refers to the injection of heroin directly into a vein.

**morphine:** An organic compound (alkaloid) found in the *Papaver somniferum* (opium poppy). Morphine must first be extracted from opium.

**opium:** A bitter, yellowish brown, naturally occurring addictive narcotic derived from the dried latex juice of the opium poppy, *Papaver somniferum*. It is the source of morphine and heroin.

**opium, prepared:** Opium that has been taken in the raw state and dissolved in hot water in order to remove impurities and vegetable matter. It is then heated to reduce its water content. As the solution cools, the opium reverts to a solid. Most opium smokers prefer to smoke prepared opium. It is also known as cooked opium, processed opium, and smoking opium.

**opium, raw:** Opium that has not been "cooked." Often contains plant scrapings, leaf pieces, and other impurities. It is also known as opium gum, crude opium, and opium sap.

**poppy:** The opium poppy, *Papaver somniferum*, is an annual plant with grayish green leaves and variously colored flowers.

**poppy pod:** The mature ovary of the opium poppy plant. It is sometimes called the seedpod, capsule, bulb, or head. It refers to the egg-size fruit that enlarges as the flower petals fall from the plant. The ovarian wall produces the white latex (opium).

**poppy pod, scoring:** The cutting into the surface of an opium poppy pod, using a sharp-bladed instrument, in order to allow the opium to exude from the pod. It is also known as lancing, incising, or tapping.

**poppy pod, scraping:** The collecting of gummy opium from the pod surface using a flat-bladed instrument. The instrument resembles a paint scraper.

**precursor:** A chemical that is the raw material for a new product. Morphine is a precursor in the production of heroin.

**skin-popping:** This refers to the injection of heroin into the skin.

# APPENDIX

## Facts About Opiates

Opiates are drugs containing opium or its derivatives. Opium is produced from the gummy substance extracted from the seedpod of the Asian poppy, *Papaver somniferum*, and is the crudest and least potent of the opiates.

Opiates are primarily central nervous system (CNS) depressants and narcotic analgesics (painkillers).

Opiates have been used both medically and nonmedically for thousands of years. A tincture of opium called laudanum (mixture of opium and alcohol) has been widely used since the sixteenth century as a remedy for anxiety or to stop coughing and diarrhea.

In the nineteenth century opium use rose greatly in the United States due to opium-smoking Chinese immigrants as well as to the practice of giving opium intravenously to many wounded Civil War soldiers.

Opium poppies were at one time widely grown as an ornamental plant and for seeds in the United States. The possession of this plant was declared illegal by the Opium Poppy Control Act of 1942.

The opium poppy is cultivated legally today on government-regulated farms in India, Turkey, China, Commonwealth of Independent States (former Soviet Union), and Tasmania, Australia. It is cultivated illegally in Afghanistan, Burma, Colombia, Guatemala, Iran, Laos, Lebanon, Mexico, Pakistan, Vietnam, and Thailand.

Illicit opium appears either as dark brown chunks or in powder form and is generally eaten, smoked, or injected. Street names for opium are "hop" and "tar."

Raw or cooked opium contains more than thirty-five different alkaloids, including morphine, codeine, and thebaine (used to produce a variety of other opioids). Of the alkaloids, only codeine and morphine are still in widespread clinical use today. Other drugs, such as heroin, are processed from morphine or codeine.

In 1806 morphine, named after Morpheus, the Greek god of sleep, was the first alkaloid to be extracted from opium.

Morphine is found in both legally and illegally manufactured forms. Legally manufactured morphine is usually found in white to brown powdered form or in pill form. Illegally manufactured morphine is usually found in powdered form and is either sniffed, injected, or smoked.

Street names for morphine are "M," Morf, Morpho, Miss Emma, "painkillers," and "pain pills."

More than 90 percent of the morphine produced in the United States is converted into codeine. Codeine is the most widely prescribed narcotic in the United States, prescribed for both pain relief and as a cough suppressant. Codeine is a controlled substance that requires a prescription.

Street names for codeine are "T-three's" (Tylenol #3 with codeine), "schoolboy," "painkillers," "pain pills," and "cough syrup."

Heroin (diacetylmorphine), a semisynthetic opiate, is produced by chemical changes made to morphine or codeine. It was introduced in 1898 and proved to be a more potent painkiller and cough suppressant than morphine. Some doctors attempted to use heroin to combat morphine addiction.

Illicit heroin appears as a white or brownish powder. Most street preparations of heroin contain only a small percentage of the drug, as they are diluted with sugar, quinine, powdered milk, common household poisons such as strychnine, or other drugs and substances.

Heroin can be ingested in various ways. It can be dissolved in water and shot into a vein ("mainlining"), the skin ("skin-popping"), or a muscle. It can be smoked with a water pipe, a regular pipe, or mixed with tobacco. It can be inhaled as smoke through a straw or sniffed as a powder through the nose.

The increased purity of heroin has allowed it to be used in many ways and has made it more popular with teenagers, since there is no longer the stigma of a needle. This has led to an increase in overdoses among teens.

Heroin is more fat soluble than morphine and thus passes the blood-brain barrier more quickly. It therefore works more quickly but for a shorter time.

Street names for heroin include Smack, Hard Stuff, "H," Big H, Brown Sugar, Mexican Brown, China White, Crap, Horse, Junk, and Mud.

The opioids are the opiate-related synthetic drugs, such as methadone, and meperidine (Demerol). The term *opioids* also refers to the entire family of both natural opiates (drugs from the opium poppy) and synthetic opioids.

Opiate-related synthetic drugs were first developed to provide analgesics that would not produce drug dependence. However, it was
found that opioids can also be addictive. The brain produces its
own version of opiates, called endogenous opioids. These chemicals act like opiates, binding to opiate receptors. Endogenous opioids are the body's way of controlling pain and produce a pleas-
antly relaxed feeling after rigorous exercise.

**B.C.**

## 3400
The opium poppy is cultivated in lower Mesopotamia. The Sumerians refer to it as *Hul Gil*, the "joy plant."

## 1300
Egyptians cultivate opium poppies and the opium trade flourishes during the reign of Thutmose IV, Akhenaton, and King Tutankhamen.

## 1100
People on the island of Cyprus craft surgical-quality culling knives to harvest opium.

## 460
Hippocrates, the "Father of Medicine," acknowledges opium's usefulness as a narcotic.

## 330
Alexander the Great introduces opium to the people of Persia and India.

**A.D.**

## 400
Egyptian opium is introduced to China by Arab traders.

## 1000
Opium is cultivated, eaten, and drunk by all classes in India as a household remedy and given to soldiers to increase their courage. In China, the medicinal use of opium is widespread.

## 1400s–1500s
"Syrup of poppy" and other poppy preparations are commonly prepared and used medicinally by monastic communities.

## 1600s
Opium, hashish, and alcohol spread among the population of Constantinople.

# 1700
The Dutch export shipments of Indian opium to the islands of Southeast Asia and China and introduce the practice of smoking opium in a tobacco pipe to the Chinese.

# 1729
Chinese emperor Yung Cheng issues an edict prohibiting the smoking of opium and its domestic sale, except for medicinal use.

# 1793
The British East India Company establishes a monopoly on the opium trade.

# 1800s
Opium dependence increases steadily in England, Europe, and the United States, where patent medicines and opium preparations are readily available.

# 1803
Morphine, an alkaloid, is isolated from opium by German pharmacist Friedrich Wilhelm Adam Serturner.

# 1841
The Chinese are defeated by the British in the first Opium War.

# 1843
Physician Alexander Wood of Edinburgh discovers a new technique for dispensing morphine—injection with a syringe.

# 1856
The British and French engage in the second Opium War with China, and the importation of opium is legalized there.

# 1874
English chemist C.R. Wright synthesizes diacetylmorphine (heroin) by boiling morphine over a stove.

# 1895
The Bayer Company begins production of diacetylmorphine and the name "heroin" is coined.

## Early 1900s
In the United States free samples of heroin are provided to morphine addicts.

## 1910
The Chinese convince the British to discontinue the India-China opium trade after 150 years.

## 1914
The Harrison Narcotics Act is passed in the United States, regulating and imposing a tax on the sale of opium, heroin, and cocaine.

## 1940s
The region of Southeast Asia (areas of Laos, Thailand, and Burma) referred to as "The Golden Triangle" becomes a major producer in the profitable opium trade.

## 1950s
In order to contain the spread of communism, the United States forges alliances with tribes and drug warlords inhabiting the Golden Triangle, providing drug warlords and their armies with arms, ammunition, and air transport for the production and sale of opium.

## 1965–1970
The United States experiences a surge in illegal heroin as the drug is smuggled into the country during the Vietnam War. To aid U.S. allies, the Central Intelligence Agency (CIA) creates a charter airline, Air America, to transport opium from Burma and Laos.

## 1995
The Golden Triangle is the world leader in opium production, yielding twenty-five hundred tons per year.

## 1999
Afghanistan has a bumper crop of forty-six hundred tons of opium and is estimated to be the origin of 75 percent of the world's heroin.

## 2000
Taliban leader Mullah Omar bans poppy cultivation in Afghanistan, and the United Nations Drug Control Program confirms that opium production has been eradicated there.

## 2001
The United States overthrows the Taliban regime in Afghanistan, and heroin floods the Pakistan market.

## 2002
Afghanistan regains its position as the world's largest opium producer.

The editors have compiled the following list of organizations concerned with the issues debated in this book. The descriptions are derived from materials provided by the organizations. All have publications or information available for interested readers. The list was compiled on the date of publication of the present volume; the information provided here may change. Be aware that many organizations take several weeks or longer to respond to inquiries, so allow as much time as possible.

## American Council for Drug Education (ACDE)
164 W. Seventy-fourth St., New York, NY 10023
(800) 488-DRUG (3784) • fax: (212) 595-2553
Phoenix House: (212) 595-5810, ext. 7860
e-mail: acde@phoenix.org • Web site: www.acde.org

The American Council for Drug Education informs the public about the harmful effects of abusing drugs and alcohol. It gives the public access to scientifically based, compelling prevention programs and materials. ACDE has resources for parents, youth, educators, prevention professionals, employers, health care professionals, and other concerned community members who are working to help America's youth avoid the dangers of drug and alcohol abuse. Its publications include books, brochures, and fact sheets.

## Center for Substance Abuse Prevention (CSAP)
5600 Fishers Ln., Rockwall II, Suite 800, Rockville, MD 20857
(301) 443-0373
e-mail: info@samshsa.gov
Web site: www.samsha.gov/csap

The Center for Substance Abuse Prevention is a federal organization responsible for improving accessibility and quality of substance abuse prevention services. The Center develops policies, programs, and services to prevent the onset of illegal drug use. The CSAP Web site offers drug facts and statistics, information on public education and training programs, and information about its publications and videotapes.

## Centers for the Application of Prevention Technologies (CAPT)
Minnesota Institute of Public Health
2720 Hwy. 10, Mounds View, MN 55112
(800) 782-1878 • fax: (763) 427-7841
Web site: www.captus.org

CAPT seeks to bring research into practice by helping community-based organizations develop substance abuse prevention programs and policies. CAPT publishes information about substance abuse prevention, drug research, and legislation. It also offers a science-based prevention primer.

## Drug Enforcement Administration (DEA)

2401 Jefferson Davis Hwy., Alexandria, VA 22301
(202) 307-1000
Web site: www.usdoj.gov/dea

The DEA is the federal agency charged with enforcing the nation's drug laws. The agency concentrates on stopping the smuggling and distribution of narcotics in the United States and abroad. It has information on drugs and drug trafficking as well as recent cases and major operations. It offers state fact sheets, news releases, speeches, and testimony, and publishes the *Drug Enforcement Magazine* three times a year.

## Drug Watch International

PO Box 45218, Omaha, NE 68145-0218
(402) 384-9212
Web site: www.drugwatch.org

Drug Watch International is a volunteer nonprofit drug information network and advocacy organization that promotes the creation of drug-free cultures in the world. Its Web site offers information on drugs, drug abuse, and drug legislation, and a glossary of terms.

## Lindesmith Center

70 W. Thirty-sixth St., 16th Fl., New York, NY 10018
(212) 613-8020 • fax: (212) 613-8021
Web site: www.lindesmith.org

The Lindesmith Center is a drug policy research institute. The center houses a library and information center, organizes seminars and conferences; acts as a link between scholars, government, and the media; directs a grant program in Europe; and undertakes projects on topics such as methadone policy reform and alternatives to drug testing in the workplace. The center publishes fact sheets on topics such as needle and syringe availability, drug prohibition and the U.S. prison system, and drug education.

## Narcotic Educational Foundation of America (NEFA)

28245 Crocker Ave., Suite 230, Santa Clarita, CA 91355-1201
(661) 775-6960 • fax: (661) 775-1648
e-mail: info@cnoa.org • Web site: www.cnoa.org/NEFA.htm

The Narcotic Educational Foundation of America was founded in 1924 to educate the public about the dangers of drug abuse. NEFA conducts research and has produced printed materials on aspects of drug abuse. A referral service and a speakers bureau are available. NEFA publishes pamphlets on such subjects as glue sniffing, cocaine, alcohol, amphetamines, heroin, and drug addiction, emphasizing the effects and dangers of drugs. It also publishes a series of Student Reference Sheets on topics including barbiturates, anabolic steroids, drug dependence, inhalants, PCP, prescription drugs, marijuana, and tobacco.

### National Center on Addiction and Substance Abuse at Columbia University (CASA)
633 Third Ave., 19th Fl., New York, NY 10017
(212) 841-5200 • fax: (212) 956-8020
Web site: www.casacolumbia.org

CASA is a private nonprofit organization that works to educate the public about the costs and hazards of substance abuse and the prevention and treatment of all forms of chemical dependency. The center supports treatment as the best way to reduce drug addiction. It produces publications describing the harmful effects of alcohol and drug addiction and effective ways to address the problem of substance abuse. It also publishes an annual report and newsletter.

### National Institute on Drug Abuse (NIDA)
U.S. Department of Health and Human Services
6001 Executive Blvd., Room 5213, MSC 9561, Bethesda, MD 20892-9561
(301) 443-1124
e-mail: Information@lists.nida.nih.gov
Web site: www.nida.nih.gov

NIDA supports and conducts research on drug abuse to improve addiction prevention, treatment, and policy efforts. It publishes the bimonthly *NIDA Notes* newsletter, the periodic NIDA Capsules fact sheets, and a catalog of research reports and public education materials covering such topics as the nature and extent of drug abuse.

### Office of National Drug Control Policy (ONDCP)
Executive Office of the President
Drugs and Crime Clearinghouse
PO Box 6000, Rockville, MD 20849-6000
(800) 666-3332 • fax: (301) 519-5212
e-mail: ondcp@ncjrs.org
Web site: www.whitehousedrugpolicy.gov

The Office of National Drug Control Policy is responsible for formulating the government's national drug strategy and the president's antidrug policy as well as coordinating the federal agencies responsible for stopping drug trafficking. It provides fact sheets and information on drugs. Drug policy studies are available upon request.

### Partnership for a Drug-Free America
405 Lexington Ave., Suite 1601, New York, NY 10174
(212) 922-1560 • fax: (212) 922-1570
Web site: www.drugfreeamerica.org

The Partnership for a Drug-Free America is a nonprofit organization that utilizes media communication to reduce demand for illicit drugs in America. Best known for its national antidrug advertising campaign, the partnership works to "unsell" drugs to children and to prevent drug use among kids. It publishes the annual *Partnership Newsletter* as well as monthly press releases about current events with which the partnership is involved.

## RAND Corporation

1700 Main St., PO Box 2138, Santa Monica, CA 90407-2138
(310) 393-0411 • fax: (310) 451-6996
Web site: www.rand.org

The RAND Corporation is a research institution that seeks to improve public policy through research and analysis. RAND's Drug Policy Research Center publishes information on the costs, prevention, and treatment of alcohol and drug abuse as well as on trends in drug-law enforcement. It has an extensive list of publications.

# FOR FURTHER RESEARCH

## Books

M.H. Abrams, *The Milk of Paradise: The Effects of Opium Visions on the Works of De Quincey, Crabbe, Francis Thompson, and Coleridge.* Cambridge: Harvard University Press, 1934.

John C. Ball and Carl D. Chambers, eds., *The Epidemiology of Opiate Addiction in the United States.* Springfield, IL: Charles C. Thomas, 1970.

Jack Beeching, *The Chinese Opium Wars.* Orlando, FL: Harcourt, 1977.

Patrick Biernacki, *Pathways from Heroin Addiction: Recovery Without Treatment.* Philadelphia: Temple University Press, 1983.

Jean Cocteau, *Opium: The Diary of a Cure.* London: P. Owen, 1957.

———, *Opium: The Diary of an Addict.* London: Longmans, Green, 1932.

Thomas De Quincey, *Confessions of an English Opium-Eater.* New York: Viking Penguin, 1971.

Edward Jay Epstein, *Agency of Fear: Opiates and Political Power in America.* New York: G.P. Putnam, 1977.

Peter Ward Fay, *The Opium War, 1840–1842.* Chapel Hill: University of North Carolina Press, 1975.

William Griffith, *Opium Poppy Garden: The Way of a Chinese Grower.* Berkeley, CA: Ronin, 1993.

Travis W. Hanes and Frank Sanello, *Opium Wars: The Addiction of One Empire and the Corruption of Another.* Naperville, IL: Sourcebooks, 2002.

Barbara Hodgson, *In the Arms of Morpheus: The Tragic History of Laudanum, Morphine, and Patent Medicines.* Buffalo, NY: Firefly Books, 2001.

———, *Opium: A Portrait of the Heavenly Demon.* London: Souvenir Press, 2001.

L.D. Kapoor, *Opium Poppy: Botany, Chemistry, and Pharmacology.* New York: Food Products Press, 1995.

Philip Lalander, *Hooked on Heroin.* New York: Berg, 2003.

Molly Lefebure, *Samuel Taylor Coleridge: A Bondage of Opium.* New York: Stein and Day, 1974.

Alfred Ray Lindesmith, *Opiate Addiction*. Bloomington, IN: Principia Press of Trinity University, 1947.

Alfred W. McCoy, *The Politics of Heroin in Southeast Asia*. New York: Harper and Row, 1972.

Barry Milligan, *Pleasures and Pains: Opium and the Orient in Nineteenth-Century British Culture*. Charlottesville: University Press of Virginia, 1995.

Debra Moraes and Francis Moraes, *The Little Book of Opium*. Berkeley, CA: Ronin, 2003.

Alvin Moscow, *Merchants of Heroin*. New York: Dial, 1968.

Mark Pownall, *Drugs, the Complete Story: Heroin*. Austin, TX: Steck-Vaugh, 1992.

Richard C. Stephens, *The Street Addict Role: A Theory of Heroin Addiction*. New York: State University of New York Press, 1991.

Charles E. Terry and Mildred Pellens, *The Opium Problem*. Montclair, NJ: Patterson Smith, 1970.

Nick Tosches, *The Last Opium Den*. New York: Bloomsbury, 2002.

## Periodicals

Judith Blackwell, "Drifting, Controlling, and Overcoming: Opiate Users Who Avoid Becoming Chronically Dependent," *Journal of Drug Issues*, 1983.

Jacques Bordaz and L.A. Bordaz, "Versatile Opium Poppy," *Natural History*, October 1980.

John Brown, "The Opium Wars," *Military History*, April 2004.

Lee P. Brown, "Eight Myths About Drugs," *Vital Speeches of the Day*, July 15, 1994.

Jay Cheshes, "A Drug Reporter's Strange Brew," *Columbia Journalism Review*, November/December 2002.

Jon Cohen, "HIV and Heroin: A Deadly International Affair," *Science*, September 19, 2003.

Ed D'Angelo, "The Moral Culture of Drug Prohibition," *Humanist*, September/October 1994.

John DiConsiglio, "Close-Up: Heroin," *Scholastic Choices*, April 2003.

Marcel Dufresne, "The Truth Hurts," *American Journalism Review*, January/February 2003.

Kendall Hamilton, "Back to Xanadu," *Newsweek*, August 29, 1994.

Sukanya Hantrakul, "Thailand: Death to Drug Dealers," *World Press Review*, May 2003.

Danylo Hawaleshka, "Too Many Deaths," *Maclean's*, February 25, 2002.

Constance Holden, "Opium-Free Poppy Under Study as Codeine Source," *Science*, December 26, 1975.

Bill Kurtis, "Caviar Connection (Heroin Smuggling)" *New York Times Magazine*, October 26, 1980.

Melvyn Levitsky, "Assessing the Current Trends in Opium Production and Heroin Trafficking," *U.S. Department of State Dispatch*, June 15, 1992.

William Lowther, "Needle Robs the Cradle," *Maclean's*, October 13, 1980.

Joseph O. Merrill, "Policy Progress for Physician Treatment of Opiate Addiction," *Journal of General Internal Medicine*, May 2002.

Michael Montagne, "Appreciating the User's Perspective: Listening to the 'Methadonians,'" *Substance Use and Misuse*, March 2002.

Ron Moreau and Sami Yousafzai, "Flowers of Destruction," *Newsweek*, July 14, 2003.

Tom Morganthau, "Deadly New Drug Passing as Heroin," *Newsweek*, January 5, 1981.

Ethan Nadelmann, "Addicted to Failure," *Foreign Policy*, July/August 2003.

Sohail Abdul Nasir, "Afghanistan: The More It Changes . . .," *Bulletin of Atomic Scientists*, March/April 2003.

J. Nieves and H. Holliday, "A Battle Against Addiction," *Scholastic Choices*, November/December 2003.

I.J. Poole, "Heroin Fix," *Black Enterprise*, August 1980.

Aram Roston, "Central Asia's Heroin Problem," *Nation*, March 25, 2002.

Richard Seymour, "The Bounty of the Golden Crescent," *Middle East*, July 2003.

John Strange, "Opiates: Are There Under-Utilized and Unexplored Areas of Prevention?" *Addiction*, November 1994.

Arlene B. Tickner, "Colombia and the United States: From Counternarcotics to Counterterrorism," *Current History*, February 2003.

*Time*, "New and Deadly Menace (White Heroin)," October 6, 1980.

Lally Weymouth, "Trouble Everywhere," *Newsweek*, February 10, 2003.

Helen E. White, "Thailand, Having Cut Its Opium Crop, Now Serves as Heroin Highway to West," *Wall Street Journal*, November 24, 1989.

D.A. Williams, "Heroin: Preparing for a New Invasion," *Newsweek*, March 10, 1980.

Gordon Witkin and Jennifer Griffin, "The New Opium Wars," *U.S. News & World Report*, October 10, 1994.

# Web Sites

Heroin Awareness Foundation, www.heroinhelp.net. This Web site offers information about the effects of heroin and some of the consequences of its abuse.

Information on Drugs of Abuse: Heroin, www.drugabuse.gov/Drug Pages/Heroin.html. This Web site provides articles, research reports, fact sheets, and other publications from the National Institute on Drug Abuse.

Opiates, www.sayno.com/opiates.html. This Web site offers general information about opiates and opiate abuse.

Opium and Opiates, www.erowid.org/chemicals/opiates/opiates.shtml. This Web site answers frequently asked questions about opium and opiate drugs.

The Opium Kings, www.pbs-org/wgbh/pages/frontline/shows/heroin. This Web page shares the story of filmmaker Adrian Cowell's thirty-year chronicle of Burma's heroin trade and the rise and fall of drug warlord Khun Sa.

# INDEX

addiction
  antidrug propaganda about,
    149–50
  casual use of, 153–54
  as central nervous system
    disorder, 127–34
  among Chinese immigrants,
    37–45
  to heroin, 18–19, 78–79
    in New York City, 79–80
    in 1920s, 81–92, 141–42
    in 1960s/1970s, 98–104, 114,
      142–45
  misperception about, 148–49
  to morphine, by physicians,
    46–48
  to OxyContin, 159–70
  physical dependence vs., 147,
    151–53
  prevalence of, 71, 79, 86, 106
  reasons for, in Asia, 108–109
  rehabilitation in Thailand,
    106–107
  see also treatment
addicts, 67–71, 81–87, 113, 126
administration methods, 18, 67
  of heroin, 110–14, 145–46
  hypodermic needles, 42–43,
    47–48, 65, 70, 157
  of methadone, 117, 119, 144
  of opium, 29
  smoking, 35–45, 67, 112
  snorting, 112, 113
Afghanistan, 93–94, 96–97,
  171–75, 177–79
Agrippina the Younger, 29
AIDS/HIV, 107, 124, 136, 137, 145
*Alabama Medical Journal*, 78–79
alcohol, 150, 155–56
*Alcoholism & Drug Abuse Weekly*
  (journal), 167
Allen, Nathan, 36
American Medical Association, 68,
  169
American Psychiatric Association,
  152

analgesics. *See* pain management
Anderson, G., 114
Arab traders, 29, 36
*Arrow* (ship), 33
Asia, 19
  CIA involvement in, 93–97
  heroin from, in 1990s, 112
  modern-day opiate trade in,
    171–79
Assembly of the League of Nations,
  90–91
Australia, 122–26, 138

*Bangor Daily News* (newspaper), 167
Barth, Gunther, 39
Bayer Laboratories, 73–74, 77,
  110–11
Bhumibol Adulyadej (king of
  Burma), 108
"black box" warning, 161–62
black market, 118–21, 142–44,
  162–64, 168
Blair, Tony, 145
Bloedorn, W.A., 79
Bogner, Matilda, 178
Booth, Martin, 21, 149
Brain Committee (U.K.), 142
British
  opiate revenues from colonies, 91
  Opium Wars and, 30–34, 36–37,
    64–65
  sahibs, 59
Bryce, James, 41
Buckland, Charles Edward, 49
Bureau of Narcotics and Dangerous
  Drugs, 114
Burma, 95, 105–109
Bush, George W., 174

Campbell, George, 56
Canada, 125
Canton (China), 38–39
Cavazzoni, M., 91
celebrities, heroin used by, 111
central nervous system disorder,
  127–34

*198*